Discover Sydney:

Insider Tips and Local Secrets

BY:

MICHAEL HARRIS

DISCLAIMER

This travel guide is provided for informational purposes only. The information contained herein is believed to be accurate and reliable as of the publication date, but may be subject to change. We are not making any warranty, express or implied, with respect to the content of this guide.

Users of this guide are responsible for verifying information independently and consulting appropriate authorities and resources prior to travel. We are not liable for any loss or damage caused by the reliance on information contained in this guide.

Information regarding travel advisories, visas, health, safety, and other important considerations can change rapidly. Users are advised to check for the most up-to-date information from official government and travel industry sources before embarking on any trip.

Travel inherently involves risk, and users are responsible for making their own informed decisions and accepting any associated risks.

TABLE OF CONTENTS

1. Introduction to Sydney

1.1 Overview of Sydney

Sydney, Australia's largest and most famous city, is known for its stunning natural beauty, vibrant culture, and lively atmosphere. Located on the east coast of the country in New South Wales, Sydney is a global city that blends a rich history with modern innovation.

Sydney's iconic landmarks, such as the **Sydney Opera**

House and **Sydney Harbour Bridge**, are recognized around the world and draw millions of visitors every year. But Sydney is more than just its famous sights. The city is home to beautiful beaches, such as **Bondi Beach** and **Manly Beach**, lush parks like the **Royal Botanic Garden**, and vibrant neighborhoods like **Surry Hills** and **Newtown**.

Sydney has a diverse population and is a melting pot of cultures, reflected in its food, art, and festivals. Whether you're exploring its bustling markets, dining in world-class restaurants, or relaxing on a harbor cruise, Sydney has something for every type of traveler.

The city is also known for its love of outdoor activities, with a mild climate perfect for surfing, hiking, and outdoor dining. Sydney's natural environment includes expansive beaches, verdant national parks, and a beautiful harbour, making it an excellent destination for both adventure seekers and those looking to relax.

With a year-round temperate climate, Sydney offers something unique no matter when you visit. From its thriving arts scene to its laid-back lifestyle, Sydney is a city that welcomes everyone, making it a must-visit destination in Australia.

1.2 Why Visit Sydney in 2024-2025?

Sydney continues to be one of the top destinations in the world for travelers, and 2024-2025 offers even more exciting reasons to visit. Whether you're a firsttime visitor or returning to explore more, here are some compelling reasons to consider Sydney as your next travel destination:

1. Iconic Landmarks and New Experiences

Sydney is home to some of the most famous landmarks on the planet, like the **Sydney Opera House** and the **Sydney Harbour Bridge**. In 2024-2025, these iconic structures will be even more accessible, with new experiences, including guided tours, cultural performances, and new vantage points for taking in the views. Plus, there are exciting events planned throughout the year, such as the **Vivid Sydney** festival of lights, art, and music.

2. Vibrant Events and Festivals

Sydney is known for hosting spectacular festivals throughout the year, including the **Sydney Festival**, **Sydney Gay and Lesbian Mardi Gras**, and **Vivid Sydney**. The year 2024-2025 will feature fresh new experiences and events celebrating everything from art and culture to food and fashion. These festivals bring a lively, colorful energy to the city, making it the perfect time to visit for those who enjoy cultural experiences.

3. Ideal Weather for Outdoor Activities

Sydney enjoys a temperate climate with warm summers and mild winters, making it a year-round destination. Whether you're swimming at **Bondi Beach**, surfing at **Manly**, or hiking through **Royal National Park**, Sydney's great weather means you can enjoy outdoor activities throughout the year. The cooler months, such as fall and winter, are particularly great for exploring the city without the summer crowds.

4. A Hub of Culinary Delights

Sydney's food scene is one of the most exciting in the world, from fresh seafood to international cuisines. New restaurants, pop-up markets, and food festivals in 2024-2025 will continue to elevate Sydney's reputation as a food lover's paradise. Whether you're craving innovative dining in **Surry Hills**, fresh fish at the **Sydney Fish Market**, or a meal with a view of the **Harbour Bridge**, there's always something new and delicious to try.

5. Sustainable and Eco-Friendly Travel Options

Sydney has embraced sustainable tourism and is making strides in eco-friendly practices. In 2024-2025, you can visit more green spaces, stay in eco-friendly accommodations, and take part in tours that focus on protecting the environment. Sydney's commitment to sustainability ensures that your visit is not only fun but also responsible.

6. Family-Friendly Adventures

For families, Sydney offers a wide range of attractions that will keep everyone entertained. From the **Taronga Zoo** and **Aquarium** to the **Sydney Tower Eye** and **Luna Park**, there's no shortage of family-friendly activities. The city also offers plenty of outdoor spaces, such as **Centennial Park** and **Sydney's beaches**, making it an excellent destination for traveling with kids.

7. A Blend of Modernity and Nature

Sydney is unique in that it offers a blend of urban excitement and natural beauty. You can explore the city's buzzing shopping districts, rooftop bars, and world-class museums, all while being just minutes away from nature reserves, beautiful beaches, and scenic parks. In 2024-2025, new walking trails, cycling paths, and conservation projects will make it even easier to connect with nature.

Sydney in 2024-2025 will offer visitors a perfect mix of iconic sights, cultural events, natural beauty, and outdoor adventures. Whether you're looking for an action-packed vacation or a relaxing retreat, Sydney provides everything you need to make your trip unforgettable.

1.3 Sydney's Climate and Seasons

Sydney enjoys a temperate climate, which makes it a great destination year-round. The city's weather is typically mild and pleasant, with warm summers and mild winters. Understanding Sydney's climate and seasons will help you plan your trip and ensure you get the most out of your visit.

Summer (December to February)

Summer in Sydney is warm and sunny, with average temperatures ranging from **21°C (69°F)** at night to **26°C (79°F)** during the day. It's the perfect time to visit if you enjoy beach activities like surfing, swimming, and sunbathing. Popular beaches like **Bondi** and **Manly** are bustling with tourists and locals alike. However, it's also the peak tourist season, so expect higher hotel prices and larger crowds at major attractions and beaches.

What to pack: Light, breathable clothing, sunscreen, swimwear, and sunglasses. Don't forget a hat and water bottle to stay hydrated.

Autumn (March to May)

Autumn is one of the best times to visit Sydney, as the weather is still warm but more comfortable, with temperatures ranging from **14°C (57°F)** at night to **22°C (72°F)** during the day. The city's parks and gardens, like the **Royal Botanic Garden** and **Hyde Park**, showcase beautiful fall foliage, creating picturesque views. Autumn also marks the start of the cultural season in Sydney, with festivals and events, such as **Vivid Sydney** (which typically takes place in May and June).

What to pack: Light layers for the day, but a light jacket for the cooler evenings. Comfortable shoes for walking around the city and exploring parks.

Winter (June to August)

Winter in Sydney is mild compared to many other global cities, with temperatures ranging from **8°C (46°F)** at night to **17°C (63°F)** during the day. While it's too cool for a beach holiday, winter is ideal for exploring Sydney's urban attractions, enjoying cozy cafes, or visiting museums and galleries. The winter months also see fewer tourists, meaning attractions like the **Sydney Opera House** and **Sydney Harbour Bridge** are less crowded, allowing for a more relaxed experience.

What to pack: A warm jacket, layers, and closed-toed shoes. Sydney can occasionally experience rainfall in winter, so bring an umbrella or raincoat.

Spring (September to November)

Spring is another fantastic season to visit Sydney. With temperatures ranging from **12°C (54°F)** at night to **22°C (72°F)** during the day, the weather is mild and pleasant, making it perfect for outdoor activities like hiking, coastal walks, and exploring the city's gardens. The blooming flowers in places like the **Royal Botanic Garden** and **Sydney's parks** add a touch of color to the city. Spring also brings a variety of events, including food and arts festivals.

What to pack: Comfortable clothing for warm days, but bring a jacket or sweater for the cooler evenings. Light rain gear might come in handy, as occasional showers are common in this season.

Rainfall

Sydney receives moderate rainfall throughout the year, with the wettest months being **February** and **June**. However, rain showers are typically short, and the city's temperate climate means it rarely gets cold enough to snow. Even during the wetter months, you'll still enjoy plenty of sunny days, so it's always a good idea to pack an umbrella or a light rain jacket just in case.

Overall Summary

Best Time to Visit: Autumn (March to May) and Spring (September to November) are the most comfortable times to visit Sydney, with mild temperatures, fewer crowds, and a variety of events and festivals.

Summer is perfect for beach lovers, but be prepared for higher crowds and temperatures.

Winter offers a quieter, more relaxed experience, with fewer tourists and mild weather, making it great for exploring the city's attractions without the crowds.

No matter when you visit, Sydney's diverse climate ensures that there's always something to enjoy in this dynamic city.

2. Planning Your Trip to Sydney

2.1 Best Times to Visit Sydney

When planning a trip to Sydney, the timing of your visit can make a big difference in the type of experience you'll have. Sydney offers a variety of attractions and activities throughout the year, and the best time to visit largely depends on your interests. Here's a breakdown of the best times to visit based on the season and what you want to do:

1. Best for Outdoor Activities and Festivals: Autumn (March to May)

Autumn is one of the most popular times to visit Sydney, offering a perfect balance of pleasant weather and fewer crowds. With mild temperatures, ranging from **14°C (57°F)** in the evenings to **22°C (72°F)** during the day, you'll find it comfortable for exploring Sydney's outdoor attractions, like hiking in **Royal National Park**, enjoying a picnic in **Centennial Park**, or cycling around **Bondi Beach**.

Why Visit in Autumn:

Ideal for outdoor activities like hiking, cycling, and coastal walks.

Vibrant cultural festivals, such as **Vivid Sydney** (in late May to June), a light, art, and music festival that turns the city into a dazzling display of creativity.

The cooler temperatures make it a great time to explore Sydney's parks and gardens, which are also stunning as they transition into autumn colors.

Fewer tourists than in summer, meaning less crowded attractions and more availability of accommodation.

2. Best for Beach Lovers: Summer (December to February)

If your goal is to enjoy Sydney's world-famous beaches, summer is the time to visit. The city is bustling with energy, and the warm weather, with temperatures ranging from **21°C (69°F)** at night to **26°C (79°F)** during the day, makes it perfect for surfing, swimming, and sunbathing at iconic spots like **Bondi Beach**, **Manly Beach**, and **Coogee Beach**.

Why Visit in Summer:

Ideal for enjoying the beautiful beaches, water sports, and outdoor festivals.

Warm weather means you can swim, surf, or simply relax by the water.

The city is filled with summer festivals, like the **Sydney Festival** and **New Year's Eve celebrations**, which include spectacular fireworks displays over **Sydney Harbour**.

Sydney's outdoor cafes and beachside bars are perfect for enjoying the sunny weather.

Drawbacks:

It is Sydney's peak tourist season, meaning larger crowds and higher hotel prices. Be sure to book accommodation in advance to avoid high costs.

3. Best for Mild Weather and Fewer Crowds: Spring (September to November)

Spring is another wonderful time to visit Sydney, with mild temperatures ranging from **12°C (54°F)** at night to **22°C (72°F)** during the day. The weather is warm but not too hot, making it great for sightseeing, visiting the **Royal Botanic Garden**, or taking a ferry to **Manly** or **Taronga Zoo**.

Why Visit in Spring:

Perfect weather for outdoor activities like coastal walks, visits to nature reserves, and sightseeing around the city.

Fewer tourists than during the summer, so you can enjoy Sydney's attractions without the long lines or crowded spaces.

Spring brings blooming flowers and beautiful scenery, especially in places like **The Royal Botanic Garden** and **Sydney's other parks**.

Popular events like **Sydney's Food Festival** and **Sydney's Lantern Festival** make it a great time for food lovers and culture seekers.

4. Best for a Quieter Experience: Winter (June to August)

While Sydney's winters are mild compared to many other places, the cooler months still offer a great opportunity to explore the city without the crowds.

With temperatures ranging from **8°C (46°F)** at night to **17°C (63°F)** during the day, winter is perfect for museum visits, enjoying cozy cafes, and taking in Sydney's indoor attractions.

Why Visit in Winter:

Fewer tourists mean you can enjoy Sydney's iconic landmarks like the **Sydney Opera House** and **Sydney Harbour Bridge** with fewer crowds.

Lower prices for accommodation and flights compared to the peak summer season.

Sydney's winter offers a more relaxed pace for exploring, with plenty of cultural events, theater performances, and museum exhibitions.

Ideal for city-based activities like visiting galleries, enjoying rooftop bars with heaters, or watching theater performances at the **Sydney Theatre Company**.

Drawbacks:

Not ideal for beach or water activities, as it can be too cool for swimming and surfing.

Some outdoor attractions may be less enjoyable in colder weather, but you can still explore many indoor cultural spots.

5. Special Events and Festivals

Sydney hosts a range of events throughout the year, so depending on your interests, you may want to plan your trip around a specific festival or celebration:

Vivid Sydney (May-June): A stunning light, art, and music festival that transforms the city into a colorful spectacle.

Sydney Festival (January): A month-long festival featuring music, theater, and dance performances.

Sydney Gay and Lesbian Mardi Gras (February/March): A world-famous event celebrating LGBTQ+ culture with parades, performances, and parties.

Overall Best Time to Visit:

Autumn and **Spring** are the best times to visit Sydney for mild weather, fewer crowds, and a wide range of outdoor activities.

Summer is perfect for those who want to experience Sydney's beaches and lively festivals but be prepared for higher crowds and prices.

Winter offers a quieter, more affordable experience with a focus on indoor attractions and cultural events.

By considering these factors, you can choose the perfect time to visit Sydney that aligns with your interests and travel goals.

2.2 Getting to Sydney: Airports and Transportation Options

Getting to Sydney is easy thanks to its modern international and domestic airports, which connect the city to destinations all around the world. Once you arrive, you'll find plenty of transportation options to help you get around the city efficiently and comfortably.

Sydney's Airports

1. Sydney Kingsford Smith Airport (SYD)
Sydney's primary airport is **Kingsford Smith Airport (SYD)**, located about **8 kilometers (5 miles)** south of the city center. It's one of the busiest airports in the world and serves both international and domestic flights. The airport consists of three terminals:

Terminal 1 (International): Handles all international flights, including those from airlines like **Qantas**, **Emirates**, **Singapore Airlines**, and **Cathay Pacific**. It offers a range of amenities, including duty-free shopping, lounges, and plenty of food options.

Terminal 2 (Domestic): Services flights from domestic airlines like **Jetstar**, **Virgin Australia**, and **Rex**.

Terminal 3 (Domestic): Primarily used by **Qantas** for domestic flights, though some **Jetstar** flights also operate from here.

How to Get to the City from the Airport:

Airport Train (Airport Link): The Airport Link train connects the airport to the city center in just **13 minutes**. It departs every **10 minutes**, and you can catch it directly from both international and domestic terminals. A one-way trip costs around **AUD $19.40** for adults (prices may vary, check before travel).

Taxis and Ride-Sharing: Taxis are readily available at the airport. A taxi to the city center will take about **20-30 minutes** depending on traffic and cost around **AUD $45-60**. Ride-sharing services like **Uber**, **Ola**, and **DiDi** are also available at the airport, with prices similar to taxis.

Shuttle Services: Shared shuttle buses operate from the airport to various locations in the city, with tickets typically costing around **AUD $18-25** per person. While not as fast as a taxi, shuttle services are often more affordable.

Car Rentals: If you prefer to drive, you can rent a car from one of the many rental agencies located at the airport. Major rental companies like **Avis**, **Hertz**, **Europcar**, and **Budget** have counters in the **Car Rental Terminal** (adjacent to the airport).

Public Buses: Public buses also serve the airport, providing an economical option to get to various parts of Sydney. Bus routes **400** and **420N** run between the airport and central Sydney. The fare is generally around **AUD $4.50**, and buses operate throughout the day and night.

2. Other Airports in Sydney

While Kingsford Smith is the main airport, Sydney is also served by **Bankstown Airport** (located 30 kilometers southwest of the city), which mainly handles general aviation, charter flights, and regional services. However, this airport is less commonly used by international or domestic travelers.

Transportation Options Within Sydney

Once you've arrived in Sydney, getting around the city is straightforward. Here are some of the best ways to travel within Sydney:

1. Public Transport: Trains, Buses, and Ferries Sydney has an extensive public transport network that includes trains, buses, and ferries. The **Opal card** is the best way to pay for all these services. It's a contactless smart card that can be used to pay for trips on trains, buses, ferries, and even some light rail services.

Trains: Sydney's train system is efficient and connects the airport with the central business district (CBD) and other suburbs. The **City Circle** train line connects key attractions like **Circular Quay**, **Darling Harbour**, and **Central Station**.

Buses: Buses are the most common way to travel short distances within the city. There are several bus routes connecting neighborhoods, shopping districts, and tourist attractions.

Ferries: Sydney's ferry system is an iconic way to get around, especially for scenic views of **Sydney Harbour**. The **Circular Quay** ferry terminal connects to destinations like **Manly**, **Taronga Zoo**, and **Balmain**.

Opal Card Prices:

Train fares range from **AUD $2.80 to $5.50** depending on distance.

Bus fares are generally **AUD $2.20 to $4.50**.

Ferry rides cost between **AUD $6 and $7** for a oneway trip to places like **Manly** or **Taronga Zoo**.

2. Ride-Sharing and Taxis

Uber, Ola, and DiDi: Ride-sharing services are widely available throughout Sydney. Prices vary based on the distance and time of day but are typically cheaper than taxis. You can download the Uber or other apps to book a ride.

Taxis: You can hail a taxi from the street or use a taxi app like **Ola** or **Silver Service**. The fare to the city center from the airport costs approximately **AUD $4560**, depending on the traffic.

3. **Bicycles and E-Scooters** Sydney is becoming more bike-friendly, with dedicated bike lanes and rental services available. You can rent bikes or **escooters** using apps like **Lime** and **Razor**, which operate throughout the city. This is a great option if you want to explore **Sydney's beaches** or parks.

4. **Car Rentals** If you plan on traveling outside of Sydney or want more flexibility, renting a car is a good option. Sydney has several car rental agencies, including **Avis**, **Budget**, **Hertz**, and **Europcar**. However, be aware that parking in central Sydney can be expensive and finding a space can be challenging, especially in popular areas like the CBD and beaches.

5. **Walking** Sydney is a very walkable city, especially in areas like the **CBD**, **Circular Quay**, **Darling Harbour**, and **The Rocks**. Many of the city's top attractions, including the **Sydney Opera House**, **Harbour Bridge**, and **Royal Botanic Gardens**, are within walking distance of each other.

Final Tips for Getting to Sydney:

Plan your arrival at **Sydney Kingsford Smith Airport (SYD)** for the easiest and most direct access to the city.

Public transport, especially the **Opal card**, is the most convenient and cost-effective way to get around Sydney.

If you're staying in central Sydney, walking and using public transport will likely be all you need to explore the city.

Always check the schedules for trains, buses, and ferries in advance, as they can vary depending on the day and time of year.

Getting to and around Sydney is simple, whether you're taking a flight, using public transportation, or renting a car. Once you're in the city, you'll find it easy to explore and enjoy everything this vibrant, beautiful city has to offer.

2.3 Getting Around Sydney: Public Transport, Rental Cars, and Walking

Sydney is a large, bustling city, but it offers many convenient options for getting around, whether you prefer using public transport, renting a car, or exploring on foot. Here's a breakdown of the best ways to navigate the city.

1. Public Transport: Trains, Buses, Ferries, and Light Rail

Sydney boasts a comprehensive public transport system that includes trains, buses, ferries, and light rail. It's easy to use and is the most common way for both locals and visitors to get around.

Opal **Card**

The **Opal card** is the key to traveling on public transport in Sydney. It's a reloadable smart card that works for trains, buses, ferries, and light rail. The card can be purchased at train stations, online, or from convenience stores and is used for both adults and children.

Cost: Fares range depending on the distance traveled, but here are general prices:

> **Trains**: Typically between **AUD $2.80** and **AUD $5.50** for a single trip.

> **Buses**: Around **AUD $2.20** to **AUD $4.50**.

> **Ferries**: The cost of a ferry ride depends on the route, usually around **AUD $6 to $7** for oneway trips to popular spots like **Manly** or **Taronga Zoo**.

Trains

Sydney's train network is extensive and connects key parts of the city. The main train station is **Central Station**, from where trains fan out to suburbs and popular attractions. The **City Circle** route connects popular areas like **Circular Quay**, **Wynyard**, and **Town Hall**. Trains run frequently, every **5-15 minutes**, and are a fast way to travel long distances.

Travel tip: If you plan to visit outer suburbs or surrounding areas like **Blue Mountains** or **Bondi**

Junction, trains are an affordable and convenient option.

Buses

Buses cover areas that are not serviced by trains or ferries. Sydney has a vast bus network, especially in suburbs like **Paddington**, **Surry Hills**, and **Newtown**, and buses can take you to beaches, shopping districts, and parks. Buses are also great for short journeys and reaching destinations in the inner city or outer suburbs.

Travel tip: Buses run regularly but can be slower during peak hours (7:00 AM - 9:00 AM and 4:30 PM - 6:30 PM) due to traffic.

Ferries

Sydney is famous for its ferry services, which allow you to travel across the beautiful **Sydney Harbour**. Ferries depart regularly from **Circular Quay**, and routes go to popular spots like **Manly, Taronga Zoo, Balmain**, and **Circular Quay**. Riding a ferry offers stunning views of landmarks such as the **Sydney Opera House** and **Harbour Bridge**.

Travel tip: For a scenic trip, take the **Manly Ferry** or **Darling Harbour Ferry**. Ferry rides usually last between **15 and 30 minutes**, depending on the route.

Light Rail

Sydney's light rail system is another useful way to travel around the inner city. It connects areas like **Pyrmont**, **Chinatown**, and **The Star Casino**, and is a great way to get to **Darling Harbour** or the **Australian National Maritime Museum**. Light rail is fast, convenient, and a good alternative if you want to avoid crowded trains or buses.

2. Rental Cars in Sydney

While Sydney has excellent public transport, renting a car can be a good option if you want to explore more remote areas or travel outside the city. Rental cars are widely available at the **Sydney Airport** and across the city, and many car rental agencies offer competitive rates.

Major Car Rental Companies

Avis

Budget

Hertz

Europcar

Thrifty

Cost: The cost of renting a car in Sydney varies by company, car type, and time of year, but expect to pay around **AUD $40-70 per day** for a standard car. Prices may increase for SUVs or luxury vehicles.

Parking in Sydney
Parking in Sydney, especially in the city center, can be challenging and expensive. There are several parking lots around popular areas, but expect to pay **AUD $30-50 per day** for parking in the city. On-street parking is available but limited, and time restrictions apply in most places.

Travel tip: If you plan to drive outside the city or explore the beaches, it's easier to find parking in less central areas like **Bondi Beach**, **Manly**, and **Coogee**. However, driving in the city center can be stressful due to traffic and limited parking options.

3. Walking Around Sydney

Sydney is a very walkable city, and many of its most iconic attractions are within walking distance of each other, especially in the central business district (CBD) and surrounding areas. Walking is one of the best ways to explore neighborhoods, parks, shopping areas, and harborside locations.

Top Walking Areas:

Circular Quay and The Rocks: Explore the **Sydney Opera House**, **Sydney Harbour Bridge**, and enjoy the views of the harbor.

Darling Harbour: A pedestrian-friendly area with attractions like **SEA LIFE Sydney Aquarium**, **Powerhouse Museum**, and beautiful waterside promenades.

Bondi to Coogee Walk: A famous coastal walk that offers stunning ocean views and beach access, perfect for a scenic, leisurely stroll.

Royal Botanic Gardens: A peaceful place to walk, offering lush gardens with views of the **Harbour Bridge** and **Opera House**.

Travel tip: Always carry water and wear comfortable shoes, especially if you plan to walk a lot during the day, as Sydney can get hot in summer.

4. Biking and Other Active Transportation Options

Sydney is becoming more bike-friendly, with dedicated bike lanes in many parts of the city, including along **Sydney Harbour** and around popular attractions like **Sydney Park** and **Centennial Park**. If you enjoy cycling, there are plenty of bike rental options available.

Bike Rental: Services like **Lime** (e-bikes and escooters) and **BykOz** (standard bicycles) allow you to rent bikes easily via mobile apps. The cost for renting an e-scooter is about **AUD $1 to unlock** and **AUD $0.45 per minute** for riding.

Opal card: It's the best way to travel on public transport. Load it up before your trip, and you'll save money and time.

Avoid peak hours: Try to travel outside **7:00 AM - 9:00 AM** and **4:30 PM - 6:30 PM** to avoid crowds and heavy traffic.

Walking: Many of the top attractions are within walking distance of each other, so it's often the best way to get around, especially in the **CBD**.

Ride-sharing services: If you're in a rush or want a more personalized experience, services like **Uber** and **Ola** are always available.

Whether you prefer public transport, renting a car, or exploring on foot, Sydney provides a variety of ways to get around. It's a city that's easy to navigate, and you'll find that each transportation option has its own set of advantages depending on your needs and travel plans.

2.4 Important Travel Tips and Local Etiquette

When traveling to Sydney, understanding local etiquette and following some simple travel tips can enhance your experience and make your time in the city more enjoyable. Here's a guide to help you navigate Sydney like a local.

1. Respect the Local Culture and People

Sydney is a diverse, cosmopolitan city, with a mix of cultures, languages, and traditions. Australians are generally friendly and relaxed, but it's important to be respectful of their customs and values.

Politeness: Australians are known for their laid-back attitude but also value politeness. Saying **"please"** and **"thank you"** goes a long way in making good impressions.

Tipping: While tipping is not compulsory in Australia, it is appreciated for good service. A tip of **10-15%** is common in restaurants and cafes. However, it's not expected in casual settings or when you're paying for takeaway food.

Punctuality: Australians tend to be punctual, so if you have appointments, tours, or dinner reservations, it's polite to arrive on time. If you're running late, it's considerate to call ahead.

2. Personal Space and Queuing

Personal Space: Australians value personal space, and it's important to respect people's space in queues, on public transport, or in general conversations.

Queuing: Queuing is a big part of Australian culture. Whether you're waiting for a bus, buying tickets, or ordering food, always stand in line and wait your turn. Cutting in line is considered rude.

3. Public Behavior and Noise

Sydney is generally a relaxed city, but there are a few things to keep in mind about public behavior:

Quiet Public Spaces: While Sydney is known for its vibrant nightlife, it's important to be respectful in public spaces. Keep noise levels low, especially in residential areas or quiet locations like libraries, public transport, or parks.

Smoking: Smoking is prohibited in most indoor public spaces, including restaurants, cafes, and bars. You will find designated smoking areas in public places. Always check for signs indicating whether smoking is allowed.

4. Dress Code and Weather Awareness

Sydney enjoys a temperate climate, and locals tend to dress casually, but it varies depending on the occasion:

Casual Dress: During the day, especially in summer, people wear casual clothes like shorts, t-shirts, and comfortable shoes. For evenings, especially if you're heading to a restaurant or theater, dressing up a little is appropriate.

Weather-Ready: Sydney's weather can be unpredictable, so be prepared. In summer, pack sunscreen, a hat, and water to stay cool in the hot sun.

In winter, pack layers as temperatures can get cooler, especially in the evenings.

5. Understanding the "No Worries" Attitude

One of the most popular phrases you'll hear in Sydney is **"No worries"**. Australians often use this to express that something is not a problem or that everything is fine. For example, when you thank someone for help, they might reply, "No worries!" It's a sign of the easygoing attitude that is prevalent in Sydney.

6. Using Public Transport

When using Sydney's public transport, here are a few tips to make your journey smoother:

Opal Card: Always tap on and off with your **Opal card** when using trains, buses, ferries, or light rail. This is essential for ensuring you pay the correct fare. Failing to tap off may result in being charged the maximum fare.

Give up Your Seat: On trains or buses, it's polite to give up your seat for people who may need it more, like elderly passengers, pregnant women, or those with disabilities.

Quiet Zones: On public transport, there are designated **quiet zones** on trains where you should refrain from speaking loudly or using your phone. It's a way of showing respect to other passengers. 7. Water Safety and Beaches Etiquette

Sydney is famous for its beaches, and knowing beach etiquette can make your visit more enjoyable and safe:

Swim Between the Flags: When swimming at the beach, always swim between the red-and-yellow flags. These areas are patrolled by lifeguards, ensuring that it's the safest spot to swim.

Respect the Lifeguards: Lifeguards are serious about beach safety in Sydney. If they ask you to leave the water or follow a certain rule, always listen.

Sun Protection: The Australian sun is intense, so always wear sunscreen, a hat, and sunglasses when outdoors. Locals are highly aware of sun safety and take precautions to avoid sunburns.

8. Respect for Wildlife and Nature

Sydney is surrounded by natural beauty, from its beaches to its national parks. Here are some ways to show respect for nature:

Don't Feed Wild Animals: While it might be tempting to feed the local wildlife, such as birds or kangaroos, it's important not to do so. Feeding wild animals can interfere with their natural diet and behaviors.

Respect National Parks: If you visit **Royal National Park** or other natural reserves, follow marked trails, avoid littering, and respect the environment to help preserve Sydney's wildlife and greenery.

9. Dining Etiquette

Food plays an important role in Sydney's culture. When dining out, there are a few things to keep in mind:

Tipping: As mentioned earlier, tipping is not compulsory but appreciated in restaurants. A tip of **1015%** is usual if the service is good. For cafes or casual eateries, tipping is optional, and rounding up the bill is common.

BYO (Bring Your Own): In Sydney, it's common for some restaurants (especially those outside the city center) . Be sure to check the policy before you go, and be aware that there may be a corkage fee (usually **AUD $10-$20** per bottle).

10. Safety and Security

Sydney is a generally safe city, but there are some common-sense tips to ensure your safety:

Stay Vigilant in Crowded Areas: Like any major city, it's important to be aware of your surroundings, especially in crowded places like shopping malls, train stations, or tourist attractions.

Emergency Numbers: In case of emergency, dial **000** for police, fire, or ambulance. This is the universal emergency number in Australia.

By following these simple travel tips and understanding local etiquette, you can make the most of your trip to Sydney. Whether you're navigating the city's public transport, respecting local customs, or enjoying the many outdoor activities, being considerate and mindful of Sydney's culture will ensure that you have an enjoyable and hassle-free visit.

3. Top Destinations in Sydney

3.1 Sydney Opera House

The **Sydney Opera House** is one of the most iconic landmarks in Australia and is internationally recognized for its unique architectural design and cultural significance. Located at Bennelong Point on Sydney Harbour, this world-renowned venue is not just a symbol of Sydney but a center for performing arts and cultural expression.

1. Architectural Wonder

Designed by Danish architect **Jørn Utzon**, the Opera House's sail-like design is instantly recognizable. Its striking white shells look like sails of a ship, and they seem to rise up from the harbor, creating an image that's as much a part of Sydney's identity as the Harbour Bridge. The building opened in **1973**, and it remains a masterpiece of modern architecture.

Key Features:

The **roof shells** are made from white ceramic tiles that shimmer in the sun.

The **concert hall** inside has some of the world's best acoustics, while the **Drama Theatre** offers intimate spaces for performances.

The **forecourt** offers one of the most breathtaking outdoor spaces in Sydney, with views of the Harbour Bridge and the city skyline.

2. Performances and Events

The Opera House is not just a pretty building — it is an active venue for arts and culture. It hosts over **1,500 performances** annually, including concerts, operas, theatre productions, dance performances, and more.

Popular Shows: The Opera House is home to the **Australian Ballet**, the **Sydney Symphony Orchestra**, and the **Opera Australia**. It's also a venue for international acts and performances, from rock bands to stand-up comedy and theater productions.

Annual Festivals: The Opera House is a central hub during **Vivid Sydney**, an annual festival of lights, music, and ideas, where the building itself becomes part of the light display.

3. Guided Tours and Experiences

If you're interested in learning about the history, architecture, and operations of this world-class building, you can take a **guided tour**. There are several tour options available:

Sydney Opera House Guided Tour: This 1-hour tour takes you behind the scenes to explore the history, architecture, and stories of the venue. You'll visit the Concert Hall, Drama Theatre, and see the areas not open to the public.

Backstage Tour: For a deeper dive into the world of performance, the **backstage tour** allows you to explore areas like dressing rooms and the stage.

Self-Guided Audio Tour: If you prefer to explore at your own pace, you can opt for an audio tour that guides you through the history and architectural details.

4. Dining and Shopping

The Opera House is more than just a place to watch performances; it also offers plenty of dining and shopping options for visitors.

Dining: There are several cafes and restaurants on the Opera House grounds, offering stunning views of the harbor. **Bennelong**, the fine dining restaurant located inside the Opera House, is known for its modern Australian cuisine and exceptional views. For something more casual, the **Opera Bar** offers a fantastic outdoor experience right on the water, ideal for enjoying a drink while watching the sunset.

Shopping: The Opera House also has a **gift shop** where you can buy a range of souvenirs, including unique Australian art, designer products, and Opera House-branded merchandise.

5. Visiting Tips

Tickets: If you're attending a performance, it's recommended to book tickets in advance, especially for popular shows. Tickets for guided tours are also available online.

> Prices for guided tours typically range from **AUD $42-$45** for adults, with discounts for students, children, and seniors.

> Ticket prices for performances vary depending on the show but typically start around **AUD $50-$100**.

Accessibility: The Opera House is fully accessible, with ramps, lifts, and hearing loops available for those with mobility or hearing impairments. There are also accessible toilets throughout the building.

Best Time to Visit: The Opera House is a must-see all year round, but visiting during the **Vivid Sydney Festival** (typically in May-June) is a special experience, with the building illuminated by spectacular light installations.

6. Why It's Worth Visiting

The Sydney Opera House offers visitors a unique combination of history, culture, and stunning architecture. Whether you're catching a world-class performance or simply soaking in the beauty of its exterior from the steps, a visit to this iconic building is an essential part of any trip to Sydney. The Opera

House not only represents Australia's rich cultural heritage but also continues to be a world leader in the arts, attracting millions of visitors every year.

3.2 Sydney Harbour Bridge

The **Sydney Harbour Bridge** is another one of the city's most iconic landmarks. Known locally as the "**Coathanger**" because of its distinctive shape, this bridge spans **Sydney Harbour** and connects the **Sydney Central Business District (CBD)** to the **North Shore**. It's not only a crucial piece of infrastructure but also a symbol of Sydney and an unforgettable sight for visitors.

1. Engineering Marvel

Opened in **1932**, the Sydney Harbour Bridge was once the largest steel arch bridge in the world. The bridge itself is 1,149 meters long and stands 134 meters above the harbor, offering stunning views of the city, opera house, and surrounding coastline.

Construction: The bridge was built during the Great Depression, employing thousands of workers who endured dangerous conditions to complete this massive project.

Materials: The bridge uses over 6 million handdriven rivets and 52,800 tons of steel, making it an engineering wonder of its time.

2. Walking and Cycling Across the Bridge

One of the best ways to experience the Sydney Harbour Bridge is by walking or cycling across it. The **pedestrian and cyclist paths** run along both sides of the bridge, offering fantastic views of the harbor and the Sydney Opera House.

Walking: It takes around **30 minutes** to walk from one end of the bridge to the other. During your walk, you'll get panoramic views of Sydney's skyline, the Opera House, and the bustling harbour.

Cycling: For those who prefer cycling, the bridge offers a dedicated path for bikes, making it an excellent way to take in the scenery while enjoying some exercise.

3. BridgeClimb Experience

For an unforgettable experience, you can take the **BridgeClimb**. This guided adventure takes you to the top of the Sydney Harbour Bridge, 134 meters above the water, where you'll enjoy 360-degree views of Sydney and beyond.

Climb Options: There are several climbing options available:

> **BridgeClimb Express**: A shorter climb, taking about **2 hours**.

> **BridgeClimb Summit**: The full experience, lasting about **3.5 hours**, where you reach the

highest point of the bridge and enjoy incredible views.

Prices: The **BridgeClimb** experience starts at around **AUD $200-$350**, depending on the time of day and the type of climb you choose.

What to Expect: You'll be provided with a jumpsuit, harness, and safety equipment, and your guide will share interesting facts and stories about the bridge's history and the surrounding area.

4. The Pylon Lookout

For those who prefer a less physically demanding experience but still want amazing views of Sydney Harbour, the **Pylon Lookout** is a great option. Located at the **south-eastern base** of the bridge, this small museum and observation deck offers breathtaking views without the need for a climb.

Museum: The museum inside the pylon showcases the history of the bridge, including its construction and the workers who built it. You'll also find exhibits about the engineering behind the bridge, with photos and artifacts that tell the story of this landmark.

Cost: Entry to the Pylon Lookout is much more affordable compared to the BridgeClimb, with tickets priced at around **AUD $20** for adults.

5. Sydney Harbour Bridge at Night

The Sydney Harbour Bridge is stunning during the day, but it's equally impressive at night. After the sun sets, the bridge lights up with a spectacular display, creating an unforgettable silhouette against the Sydney skyline. The city's lights reflect off the water, making it a favorite time for photographers and visitors looking to capture the beauty of Sydney.

Best Viewpoints: Some of the best places to view the Sydney Harbour Bridge at night include:

Circular Quay: Located near the Opera House, this area offers great views of both the bridge and the harbor.

Kirribilli: On the North Shore, this area provides a great perspective of the bridge lit up at night.

6. Accessibility and Visitor Information

Getting There: The bridge is easily accessible by public transport, including **train, bus, and ferry** services that all stop near the bridge. The **Milsons Point** and **North Sydney** train stations are located just a short walk from the northern side of the bridge.

Opening Hours: The Sydney Harbour Bridge is open to pedestrians and cyclists 24/7. However, for the BridgeClimb, it's best to check availability in advance, as it requires bookings.

7. Why It's Worth Visiting

The Sydney Harbour Bridge offers not only a critical connection between the city's two sides but also an unforgettable experience for visitors. Whether you're walking across the bridge, taking in the views from the Pylon Lookout, or challenging yourself with the BridgeClimb, this landmark should be on every Sydney visitor's list. With its rich history, stunning views, and unique experiences, the Sydney Harbour Bridge is a must-see during any trip to the city.

3.3 Bondi Beach and Coastal Walks

Bondi Beach is one of Sydney's most famous beaches and a top destination for both locals and tourists. Known for its golden sands, great surf, and vibrant atmosphere, Bondi Beach is an essential part of Sydney's identity. It's also the starting point for one of the most scenic coastal walks in the world.

1. Bondi Beach: A Sydney Icon

Bondi Beach is located about 7 kilometers east of Sydney's Central Business District (CBD) and is easily accessible by public transport, including buses and trains.

The Beach: Bondi is a popular spot for sunbathing, swimming, surfing, and people-watching. The beach is patrolled by lifeguards, making it safe for swimmers, but it's essential to always follow safety warnings about currents and surf conditions.

Surfing: Bondi Beach is one of the best places in Sydney for surfers, whether you're a beginner or an experienced surfer. The waves here can range from gentle to more challenging, making it a great spot for surf lessons. There are several surf schools on the beach where you can rent equipment and take lessons.

>   **Surf Schools**: Prices for lessons typically range from **AUD $50-$120** for a group lesson and **AUD $100-$180** for a private lesson.

Amenities: Bondi Beach offers all the necessary facilities for a comfortable beach day, including showers, toilets, and plenty of cafes and restaurants. You can grab a bite to eat at **Bondi Icebergs Club**, which offers excellent views of the beach, or check out the trendy cafes along **Bondi Road**.

2. Bondi to Coogee Coastal Walk

The **Bondi to Coogee Coastal Walk** is one of Sydney's most famous walks, offering stunning views of the Pacific Ocean, cliffs, beaches, and coves. It's a must-do for nature lovers and those who want to experience Sydney's coastline up close.

Distance and Duration: The walk is about **6 kilometers (3.7 miles)** long and takes around **2 to 3 hours** to complete, depending on how many stops you make along the way.

Difficulty: The walk is generally easy and wellmaintained, with some moderate inclines. It's suitable for most fitness levels, but wear comfortable shoes as some sections can be rocky.

Highlights of the Walk:

Tamarama Beach: Known as "Glamarama," this small beach is known for its beautiful scenery and surfing conditions.

Bronte Park: A lovely park perfect for a rest stop, with large open spaces, picnic spots, and a great swimming pool for families.

Clovelly Beach: A small, calm beach popular with snorkelers because of its clear water and marine life.

Gordons Bay: A peaceful cove known for its underwater life, perfect for a swim or snorkel.

Coogee Beach: The end of the walk is at Coogee Beach, a lively area with cafes, restaurants, and a great place to relax after the walk.

Things to Know:

Entrance Points: The walk starts at **Bondi Beach** and ends at **Coogee Beach**, but it can be done in either direction. It's best to start early in the day to avoid the heat and crowds.

Snacks and Water: There are plenty of places to buy snacks, drinks, and food along the walk, but it's a good idea to bring water and a snack to keep you energized.

Accessibility: Parts of the walk may not be suitable for strollers or wheelchairs due to uneven terrain, but there are some accessible areas along the route.

3. Other Coastal Walks Around Bondi

Bondi Beach is also close to other coastal walks that offer equally stunning views of the ocean and surrounding areas:

Bondi to Watsons Bay Walk: This walk is a longer option, around **12 kilometers (7.5 miles)**, that takes you through **Coastal Cliffs**, **Redleaf Pool**, and **Rose Bay**, offering spectacular views of Sydney Harbour. It usually takes **3 to 4 hours** to complete.

Bondi to Bronte Walk: If you're looking for a shorter walk, the Bondi to Bronte stretch offers a more peaceful and picturesque experience with a 2kilometer route through coastal paths and secluded beaches.

4. Bondi Beach and the Local Culture

Bondi Beach is not just about the sand and surf; it's also a cultural hub, with a vibrant community of locals and visitors. The area around Bondi has become known for its laid-back atmosphere, stylish cafes, and eclectic mix of art galleries and shops.

Bondi Markets: Held on weekends, the **Bondi Markets** are a great place to shop for unique clothing, handmade crafts, and locally grown produce. It's a fun, community atmosphere where you can find everything from vintage clothing to organic food stalls.

Bondi's Art Scene: The Bondi area has a growing art scene, with galleries showcasing both contemporary and traditional Australian art. Some street art can also be found in the laneways and around the beach.

5. Dining and Relaxing in Bondi

After a day on the beach or a coastal walk, Bondi offers a wide range of dining options, from casual cafes to fine dining. Many of the restaurants here offer great views of the beach and are perfect for enjoying a meal after a swim or a walk.

Bondi Icebergs Club: A must-visit for both the food and the view, this iconic club offers a great restaurant and a famous ocean pool, ideal for a dip while enjoying the stunning surroundings.

Cafes and Restaurants: Bondi Road is lined with trendy cafes where you can enjoy everything from smoothie bowls to gourmet coffee. For a more substantial meal, there are plenty of restaurants offering fresh seafood and international cuisine, such as **Totti's** and **Icebergs Dining Room and Bar**.

6. Why It's Worth Visiting

Bondi Beach is more than just a beautiful beach. With its combination of vibrant culture, stunning natural beauty, and world-class walking trails, it offers something for everyone. Whether you're visiting for a few hours to soak up the sun, surfing the waves, or completing the scenic coastal walk, Bondi is an unmissable destination for any trip to Sydney.

3.4 Darling Harbour and Barangaroo

Darling Harbour and **Barangaroo** are two of Sydney's most popular waterfront destinations. Located just a short walk from the city center, these areas offer a mix of leisure, culture, dining, and stunning views, making them essential spots to visit during your trip to Sydney.

1. Darling Harbour: Sydney's Vibrant Waterfront Playground

Darling Harbour is one of Sydney's most bustling areas, perfect for a day of sightseeing, entertainment, and relaxation. It offers a variety of attractions for all ages, from world-class museums and aquariums to lush green spaces and outdoor dining.

Attractions in Darling Harbour:

Australian National Maritime Museum: This museum showcases Australia's maritime history with exhibits on naval ships, submarines, and maritime exploration. Visitors can explore real ships docked at the museum, including a replica of the **Endeavour**, Captain Cook's ship.

> **Entry Fee**: Around **AUD $25** for adults, with discounts for children and seniors.

SEA LIFE Sydney Aquarium: A fun stop for families and marine life enthusiasts, the aquarium is home to a variety of sea creatures, including sharks, stingrays, and the iconic dugongs.

> **Entry Fee**: Around **AUD $47** for adults, with discounted rates for children and families.

WILD LIFE Sydney Zoo: A chance to get close to Australian wildlife, including kangaroos, koalas, and crocodiles. The zoo offers a great introduction to the unique animals of Australia.

> **Entry Fee**: Around **AUD $42** for adults.

Cockle Bay Wharf: A great spot for dining and entertainment, with numerous restaurants and bars offering both casual and fine dining. You can enjoy seafood with a view of the harbor or have a drink in one of the trendy waterfront bars.

Public Spaces and Attractions:

Tumbalong Park: A spacious green park with playgrounds and picnic areas, perfect for families or a relaxing break. It often hosts outdoor events, markets, and concerts, especially during the warmer months.

Darling Quarter: A lively area with cafes, restaurants, and a large playground for children. It's also home to the **Monkey Baa Theatre Company**, which offers familyfriendly performances.

Dining in Darling Harbour: Darling Harbour is filled with dining options, from casual eateries to upscale restaurants. Whether you're after a coffee by the water, a family-friendly meal, or a sophisticated dinner with a view, you'll find something for every taste and budget.

Hurricane's Grill: Known for its steaks and ribs, offering a vibrant atmosphere and views of the harbor.

The Darling Hotel Restaurants: Offering luxury dining with contemporary Australian cuisine and a stunning view of the waterfront.

2. Barangaroo: Sydney's Modern Waterfront Hub

Barangaroo is a newer development in Sydney, named after the influential Aboriginal woman Barangaroo, and is a prime example of modern urban renewal. Located just north of Darling Harbour, Barangaroo combines cutting-edge architecture, green spaces, and waterfront dining. It's a great place to relax, explore, and enjoy the city's more contemporary offerings.

Barangaroo Reserve: A beautifully designed 22hectare parkland area with manicured gardens, walking paths, and stunning views of Sydney Harbour. The reserve features native plants and art installations and is perfect for a relaxing walk or a picnic.

> **Walking Trails**: The reserve includes a scenic **Barangaroo Walk**, which connects to the **Sydney Harbour Bridge** and **Circular Quay**. This walk allows you to enjoy spectacular views of the harbour and the city skyline.

> **The Cutaway**: A stunning space beneath the Barangaroo Reserve used for cultural and arts events, exhibitions, and performances. The architecture here is modern and awe-inspiring, making it a unique spot for photos.

> **Aboriginal Heritage Walk**: A guided walking tour that focuses on the cultural significance of the area to the local **Cadigal people**, who have a long connection to the land.

Barangaroo's Dining Scene: Barangaroo has quickly become known for its impressive range of restaurants and eateries, particularly those along **Wulugul Walk**, a waterfront promenade. Here, you can enjoy gourmet dining with stunning views of the harbor.

Aria Restaurant: A high-end restaurant offering contemporary Australian cuisine, with dishes created by renowned chefs. It's perfect for a special occasion or an unforgettable dining experience.

Rosetta: An Italian restaurant offering fresh pasta and sophisticated meals, located right by the water with views of the harbour.

Café Del Mar: A laid-back venue offering Mediterranean-inspired cuisine, perfect for a relaxed meal or drink by the waterfront.

Shopping in Barangaroo: Barangaroo is home to some luxury shopping destinations, including **The Streets of Barangaroo**, a retail area offering upscale shops, fashion boutiques, and local designers. It's a great place to shop for unique Australian brands or find a special souvenir.

3. How to Get to Darling Harbour and Barangaroo

Both Darling Harbour and Barangaroo are easily accessible from Sydney's city center and surrounding areas. Public transport options include:

Public Transport: Darling Harbour is a short walk from the **Town Hall** or **Central** stations, both wellserved by trains, buses, and light rail.

Light Rail: The **L1 Dulwich Hill Line** of the light rail stops at **Pyrmont Bridge**, close to Darling Harbour.

Ferry: Barangaroo is accessible by ferry from Circular Quay, with a ferry terminal located just a few minutes' walk from the Barangaroo Reserve.

Walking: These areas are within walking distance from **Circular Quay**, **The Rocks**, and **King Street Wharf**, making it easy to explore on foot.

4. Why Visit Darling Harbour and Barangaroo?

Family-Friendly: Both Darling Harbour and Barangaroo are great for families, with plenty of attractions, parks, and dining options to keep everyone entertained. The museums and the zoo in Darling Harbour are especially popular with children.

Great Views: Whether you're walking along the water or dining at a waterfront restaurant, the views of the harbor, Sydney Tower, and the city skyline are stunning and offer some of the best photo opportunities in Sydney.

Modern and Historic Blend: Darling Harbour offers a more classic, lively atmosphere with historic sites and attractions, while Barangaroo represents Sydney's modern, eco-friendly urban development. Together, these areas offer a well-rounded Sydney experience.

Visiting Darling Harbour and Barangaroo provides an exciting blend of history, modern culture, entertainment, and outdoor enjoyment, making them must-visit destinations for anyone traveling to Sydney.

3.5 The Rocks: Sydney's Historic Precinct

The Rocks is one of the oldest and most iconic areas in Sydney, offering a rich history, stunning architecture, vibrant markets, and a lively cultural scene. Located near the Sydney Harbour Bridge and Circular Quay, The Rocks is the heart of Sydney's colonial past and a must-visit for anyone interested in the city's history and character.

1. A Walk Through History

The Rocks is known as the birthplace of Sydney. It was here that the first European settlers arrived in 1788, making it the site of many important historical events. The area's cobbled streets, historic buildings, and preserved warehouses transport visitors back in time to Sydney's early days.

Historical Significance: The Rocks was originally settled by convicts, and over the years, it developed into a lively working-class area. Today, you can still see remnants of this early colonial life, from the old sandstone buildings to the narrow alleyways where workers once lived and labored.

The Rocks Discovery Museum: This small but informative museum offers a glimpse into the history of The Rocks, showcasing everything from the area's Indigenous heritage to the arrival of the First Fleet. You'll learn about the development of Sydney, the lives of early settlers, and how The Rocks evolved into the bustling part of the city it is today.

Entry Fee: Free

Location: 2-4 Circular Quay East, The Rocks 2.

Iconic Landmarks

The Rocks is home to several significant landmarks that highlight Sydney's history and culture.

Sydney Harbour Bridge: The towering **Sydney Harbour Bridge** is an iconic symbol of Australia and one of the most photographed landmarks in the country. You can walk across the bridge or take a **BridgeClimb** to the top for breathtaking views of the city and the harbour. The **BridgeClimb** is an exhilarating experience, allowing you to scale the bridge with a guide while taking in 360-degree views of the harbour.

BridgeClimb Fee: Around **AUD $174** for adults (basic experience)

Cadmans Cottage: Built in 1816, **Cadmans Cottage** is one of the oldest surviving residential buildings in Australia. It was once the home of the water police and is now a museum that offers insight into the early life of settlers and the development of Sydney's waterfront. Visitors can also enjoy the beautiful views from the cottage's garden overlooking Circular Quay.

Entry Fee: Free

Susannah Place Museum: This museum consists of a row of four historic terrace houses built in the 1840s. It offers a glimpse into the lives of working-class families who lived in The Rocks during the 19th and early 20th centuries. The museum's exhibits explore the social and cultural aspects of life in the area and provide an excellent opportunity to understand how the neighborhood evolved over time.

Entry Fee: Around **AUD $10** for adults

Location: 58-64 Gloucester Street, The Rocks

3. Markets and Shopping

The Rocks is famous for its lively markets, which showcase a mix of local crafts, artisan goods, fresh produce, and vintage items. These markets are a great place to pick up unique souvenirs, sample local food, or simply enjoy the atmosphere.

The Rocks Markets: The weekend markets (open Friday to Sunday) offer a fantastic selection of handmade jewelry, clothing, artwork, and homeware. You can also find street food vendors selling international cuisine, local delicacies, and sweet treats. The markets are a vibrant and colorful part of the area, drawing both tourists and locals alike.

Opening Hours: Friday (9 am – 3 pm), Saturday & Sunday (10 am – 5 pm)

The Rocks Village Bizarre (Seasonal Event): During the holiday season, The Rocks transforms into a festive wonderland with holiday lights, performances, and extra market stalls. It's an exciting event to visit if you're in Sydney during the Christmas season.

Retail Shopping: In addition to the markets, The Rocks also has several boutique shops selling Australian-made products, designer fashion, souvenirs, and local art. The cobblestone streets are lined with historical shops offering a variety of products, making it a fun place to explore and shop.

4. Dining and Pubs

The Rocks is also known for its fantastic selection of restaurants, pubs, and cafes, many of which have been around for decades. Whether you want a casual bite or a gourmet meal with a view, The Rocks has something to offer.

The Australian Heritage Hotel: One of the oldest pubs in Sydney, The Australian Heritage Hotel is the perfect spot to experience traditional Aussie pub food. They're particularly famous for their gourmet **pizza**

selection, with unique toppings such as kangaroo, crocodile, and emu.

Location: 100 Cumberland Street, The Rocks

The Glenmore Hotel: This historic pub features a rooftop terrace with amazing views of the Sydney Harbour Bridge. The Glenmore serves classic pub meals.

Location: 96 Cumberland Street, The Rocks

Café Sydney: For fine dining with a spectacular view, Café Sydney, located on the rooftop of Customs House, offers delicious contemporary Australian cuisine and unbeatable views of the Sydney Harbour Bridge and Opera House.

Location: Level 5, Customs House, 31 Alfred Street, Circular Quay

5. The Rocks Today: A Mix of Old and New
Today, The Rocks continues to blend its rich history with modern culture. While it retains much of its oldworld charm, the area is now home to luxury apartments, modern offices, and high-end restaurants. Its historic sites sit alongside contemporary art galleries and trendy bars, offering a mix of Sydney's past and present. The area remains a hub for both locals and visitors, with regular events, festivals, and outdoor performances that draw crowds year-round.

The Rocks Walking Tours: A great way to learn more about The Rocks is by taking a walking tour.

These tours are led by knowledgeable guides who share stories about the area's history, from its Aboriginal heritage to its colonial past.

Tour Price: Around **AUD $35** per person 6.

How to Get to The Rocks

The Rocks is centrally located and easy to reach from various parts of Sydney. It's just a short walk from Circular Quay, where you can catch ferries, trains, and buses.

Public Transport: The **Circular Quay** station is the nearest major transport hub, and it's well-served by trains, buses, and ferries. From there, you can walk to The Rocks in just a few minutes.

Walking: The Rocks is also within walking distance from **Sydney Opera House**, **Botanic Gardens**, and **Darling Harbour**.

7. Why Visit The Rocks?

Rich History: The Rocks is where Sydney's European settlement began, and its historical sites offer a fascinating glimpse into the past.

Vibrant Markets: The weekend markets and seasonal events make it a lively spot for shopping and experiencing local culture.

Dining and Pubs: With its historical pubs, trendy restaurants, and casual cafes, The Rocks is a food lover's paradise.

Picturesque Views: The area's cobbled streets, historic buildings, and views of the Sydney Harbour Bridge make it one of the most picturesque places in Sydney.

Visiting The Rocks offers an exciting opportunity to walk through Sydney's history while enjoying modernday attractions, making it an essential stop for anyone exploring Sydney.

4. Outdoor Activities in Sydney

4.1 Hiking and Coastal Walks in Sydney

Sydney is not only known for its vibrant city life and stunning landmarks, but also for its beautiful natural landscapes and outdoor activities. Whether you're a nature enthusiast or just looking to enjoy some fresh air, Sydney offers a wide variety of hiking trails and coastal walks that showcase the city's stunning scenery, from breathtaking views of the ocean to lush bushland. Here are some of the best hiking and coastal walks to explore:

1. Bondi to Coogee Coastal Walk

One of the most famous coastal walks in Sydney, the **Bondi to Coogee Walk** takes you along the city's eastern coastline, offering some of the most stunning views of the Pacific Ocean. The 6 km (3.7 miles) trail takes around 2-3 hours to complete, depending on your pace and the stops you make along the way.

Highlights: The walk passes through iconic beaches like **Bondi**, **Tamarama**, **Bronte**, and **Coogee**, offering views of the sparkling blue water, sandy shores, and rocky cliffs. There are also plenty of opportunities to stop for a swim, grab a coffee, or simply enjoy the scenery at one of the coastal parks.

Difficulty: Easy to moderate. The walk is mostly flat, but there are some steep sections near the cliffs.

Best Time to Visit: The walk can be done year-round, but it's especially popular during the warmer months (September to April).

Cost: Free

2. Manly to Spit Bridge Walk

The **Manly to Spit Bridge Walk** is a 10 km (6.2 miles) trail that offers a unique combination of stunning ocean views, bushland, and tranquil beaches. It takes about 3-4 hours to complete, making it a perfect half-day adventure.

Highlights: This walk provides fantastic views over **Sydney Harbour**, and you'll pass through **Glenrock Reserve** and **Gibson's Beach**. Along the way, you'll see a diverse mix of landscapes, from coastal bushland to quiet coves. The walk ends at the **Spit Bridge**, where you can enjoy the beautiful surroundings and catch a ferry back to Manly or Circular Quay.

Difficulty: Moderate. The track includes some steep climbs and uneven surfaces, but it's manageable for most walkers.

Best Time to Visit: Ideal for spring and autumn when the weather is mild.

Cost: Free

3. Royal National Park: The Coast Track

The **Coast Track** is one of the most scenic and challenging hikes in Sydney, located in the **Royal National Park**. This 26 km (16 miles) trail can be completed in two days, though many choose to do it as a one-day adventure. It's perfect for experienced hikers looking for a bit of a challenge.

Highlights: The Coast Track offers panoramic ocean views, as well as opportunities to spot native wildlife, including bird species and possibly even dolphins or whales. You'll pass through **Wattamolla Beach**, **Garie Beach**, and **Bundeena**, all of which are perfect for a swim or picnic. The rugged cliffs and dense bushland also make it a memorable experience.

Difficulty: Difficult. The track is long and features some steep ascents and descents, so it's better suited for seasoned hikers.

Best Time to Visit: Spring or autumn, when the weather is more temperate.

Cost: Free (but there may be a parking fee in some areas of the park).

4. Ku-ring-gai Chase National Park: Cowan to Brooklyn Walk

If you're looking for a more peaceful, nature-filled escape from the city, the **Cowan to Brooklyn Walk** in the **Ku-ring-gai Chase National Park** is a perfect option. This 6.5 km (4 miles) trail takes you through beautiful bushland and offers views of the **Hawkesbury River**.

Highlights: Along the walk, you'll pass through dense eucalyptus forests, walk over rocky outcrops, and enjoy spectacular views of the river. The area is also known for its Aboriginal heritage, and you'll find rock engravings and other cultural sites along the way.

Difficulty: Moderate. The trail has some steep sections and uneven terrain, but it's manageable for most walkers.

Best Time to Visit: Spring and autumn when the weather is pleasant and the wildflowers are in bloom.

Cost: Free

5. Sydney Harbour National Park: The Hermitage Foreshore Walk

The **Hermitage Foreshore Walk** is a 1.8 km (1.1 miles) easy, family-friendly coastal walk that takes you along the Sydney Harbour. This walk is perfect for those who want to enjoy nature without a strenuous hike.

Highlights: The walk provides stunning views of **Sydney Harbour**, **Shark Island**, and the **Opera House**, along with stops at beautiful spots like **Nielsen Park** and **Rose Bay**. The trail also includes the **Hermitage Cottage**, a historic building with ties to Sydney's colonial past.

Difficulty: Easy. This is a relatively short and flat walk, making it accessible to people of all fitness levels.

Best Time to Visit: Great year-round, especially for a scenic stroll.

Cost: Free

6. Garigal National Park: The Cascades Walk

Located in Sydney's northern suburbs, **Garigal National Park** offers the **Cascades Walk**, a 2 km (1.2 miles) trail that takes you through lush forest, along streams, and past beautiful waterfalls. It's a short but rewarding walk for those looking for a quick nature escape.

Highlights: The walk follows a series of cascades along **Lyre Bird Gully**, offering a peaceful and serene environment. You'll pass through forested areas, cross a few streams, and enjoy the sounds of nature. The walk ends at the **Cascades**, where you can rest and enjoy the scenery.

Difficulty: Easy to moderate. The trail is relatively short but can be muddy after rain, so be prepared for slippery paths.

Best Time to Visit: Spring or autumn for pleasant weather and lush surroundings.

Cost: Free

7. Tips for Hiking and Coastal Walks in Sydney

Wear Comfortable Shoes: Make sure to wear sturdy, comfortable shoes suitable for walking on rocky and uneven terrain.

Bring Water and Snacks: Sydney's coastal and bushland walks can be long, so it's important to stay hydrated and bring along a snack for energy.

Check the Weather: Sydney can be hot in summer and rainy in winter. Always check the weather forecast before you go and wear appropriate clothing.

Respect Nature: Stick to marked trails, avoid littering, and respect wildlife. Sydney's natural parks are precious, and it's important to help preserve them for future generations.

Sun Protection: Sydney is known for its strong sun, so make sure to wear sunscreen, a hat, and sunglasses for protection.

Conclusion

Sydney's hiking and coastal walks are one of the best ways to explore the city's natural beauty. Whether you're walking along the coast, through national parks, or over rugged bushland, these trails offer a diverse range of landscapes and experiences. From the iconic Bondi to Coogee walk to the more challenging Royal National Park tracks, there's something for every type of adventurer in Sydney. So, lace up your hiking boots and set out to discover the incredible outdoor wonders Sydney has to offer!

4.2 Surfing and Water Sports in Sydney

Sydney is known for its beautiful beaches, and it's no surprise that surfing and other water sports are a huge part of the city's lifestyle. Whether you're an experienced surfer or a beginner eager to catch your first wave, Sydney offers plenty of opportunities for surfing and other exciting water activities. With its sunny weather, long sandy beaches, and surf-friendly waves, Sydney is a paradise for anyone who loves the water. Here's a look at some of the best surfing spots and water sports in Sydney:

1. Bondi Beach: Surfing for All Levels

Bondi Beach is one of Sydney's most iconic beaches, and it's a hotspot for both local surfers and tourists. The beach is known for its consistent surf, which makes it ideal for surfers of all skill levels, from beginners to advanced.

For Beginners: Bondi Beach is home to several surf schools that offer lessons for beginners. These schools will teach you how to paddle, catch waves, and maintain balance on your surfboard. Expect to pay around **AUD 80-150** for a group lesson (typically 1.52 hours).

For Advanced Surfers: For more experienced surfers, Bondi offers a variety of wave conditions, ranging from gentle to more powerful waves, depending on the time of year and weather conditions.

Facilities: Bondi Beach has surfboard rentals available for around **AUD 20-40 per hour**. You'll also find plenty of cafés, showers, and surf shops to enjoy when you need a break.

Best Time to Visit: The best time for surfing at Bondi Beach is from **March to May** and **September to**

November, when the water temperature is comfortable and the surf conditions are ideal.

2. Manly Beach: A Surfer's Paradise

Another famous spot for surfing in Sydney is **Manly Beach**, located on the northern beaches. This beach is perfect for both beginners and seasoned surfers, with surf schools, gentle waves, and larger swells depending on the conditions.

For Beginners: Manly's surf schools are popular for teaching beginners, and they offer group lessons as well as private lessons. The prices are typically **AUD 80-150 per lesson** for about 1.5 hours.

For Experienced Surfers: Experienced surfers will enjoy Manly's variety of waves, with some areas offering larger swells, especially during the winter months (May-August).

Facilities: Manly Beach has excellent facilities, including rentals for surfboards (around **AUD 20-40 per hour**) and equipment, as well as cafes and shops along the beach for after-surf relaxation.

Best Time to Visit: **March to May** and **September to November** are great months for surfing, as these months offer good weather and surf conditions.

3. Maroubra Beach: A Local Surfing Gem

Maroubra Beach is located in the eastern suburbs of Sydney and is less crowded than Bondi and Manly, making it a local favorite for surfers looking for more space and fewer tourists.

For Beginners: While the waves at Maroubra can sometimes be a bit more challenging than Bondi or Manly, there are still surf schools that cater to beginners and intermediate surfers. Lessons typically cost around **AUD 80-150** for group sessions.

For Experienced Surfers: Maroubra has excellent waves for intermediate and advanced surfers, especially in the winter months when the surf conditions are more consistent.

Facilities: There are surfboard rentals available at Maroubra, generally priced at around **AUD 20-30 per hour**. The beach is also equipped with great local cafés and restaurants.

Best Time to Visit: Maroubra is great to surf yearround, but the winter months (May to August) are particularly good for more experienced surfers due to the bigger swells.

4. Cronulla Beach: Perfect for Family Surfing

Cronulla Beach is a great option for families and beginners. With plenty of surf schools and calm, gentle waves, it's a wonderful spot for learning to surf and enjoying other water activities.

For Beginners: Cronulla Beach is ideal for novice surfers, as the waves are usually smaller and easier to navigate. Surf schools in the area offer group and private lessons starting at around **AUD 70-150** per session.

For Experienced Surfers: Cronulla is also home to more advanced surf breaks, like the **Shark Island** reef break, which attracts experienced surfers.

Facilities: Surfboard rentals are available for around **AUD 20-40 per hour**, and there are many familyfriendly amenities, such as picnic areas, cafes, and change rooms.

Best Time to Visit: Cronulla is great for surfing yearround, but the summer months (December to February) offer the best conditions for beginners.

5. Surfing Lessons and Rentals

Sydney has plenty of surf schools and equipment rental shops scattered across its famous beaches. Whether you're a beginner looking to learn the ropes or an experienced surfer needing a board, you'll find everything you need.

Surf Schools: Surf schools offer beginner lessons, private coaching, group sessions, and surf camps. A typical group lesson lasts about 1.5 to 2 hours and costs around **AUD 80-150**.

Board Rentals: If you already know how to surf and just need a board, rentals are available at most beaches. Expect to pay around **AUD 20-40 per hour** or **AUD 50-80 per day** for a standard surfboard. You can also rent other equipment like wetsuits for about **AUD 1020** per hour.

Private Lessons: For one-on-one coaching, prices can range from **AUD 120 to 250 per lesson**, depending on the surf school and lesson duration.

6. Other Water Sports in Sydney

Sydney isn't just for surfing; it's also a great city for other water sports. Here are a few more activities to try:

Stand-Up Paddleboarding (SUP): SUP is a popular water sport, and you can try it at beaches like **Bondi**, **Manly**, and **Palm Beach**. Rentals for **AUD 20-40 per hour** are common.

Kayaking: Kayak rentals are available in areas like **Sydney Harbour**, where you can paddle under the **Sydney Harbour Bridge** or near **Circular Quay**. Rental prices are typically **AUD 25-50 per hour**.

Windsurfing and Kitesurfing: If you're looking for an adrenaline rush, **Botany Bay** and **Narrabeen Beach** are top spots for windsurfing and kitesurfing. Expect rental costs of around **AUD 50-90 per hour** for equipment.

Jet Skiing: For those who want a faster adventure, **Sydney Harbour** offers jet ski rentals. These can cost around **AUD 150-250 per hour**, depending on the location.

7. Surf Etiquette and Safety Tips

Respect Local Surf Etiquette: In Sydney, like everywhere else, surfers follow certain rules to make sure everyone stays safe and has a good time. Always give priority to the surfer who is closest to the breaking wave, and don't drop in on someone else's wave.

Know Your Limits: Don't try to surf on waves that are too big or challenging for your skill level. Always start with smaller waves and work your way up.

Safety First: Always wear a leash on your surfboard to prevent it from drifting away. If you're a beginner, consider taking a lesson to learn the basics of safety in the water.

Conclusion

Sydney is a world-class destination for surfing and water sports, offering a range of options for everyone, from beginners to advanced surfers. Whether you're catching waves at Bondi, learning to surf at Manly, or exploring other thrilling water activities like kayaking and paddleboarding, there's no shortage of ways to enjoy Sydney's beaches and waterways. Don't forget to respect the surf etiquette and take safety seriously, so you can enjoy all the fantastic water experiences Sydney has to offer!

4.3 Scenic Views and Lookouts in Sydney

Sydney is known for its stunning coastal landscapes, lush greenery, and breathtaking skyline. From clifftop vistas to waterfront panoramas, there are many scenic spots across the city that offer incredible views. Whether you're exploring the beaches, hiking in the national parks, or simply looking to enjoy the beauty of the city, Sydney has numerous lookout points that will leave you in awe. Here's a guide to some of the best scenic views and lookouts in Sydney:

1. Sydney Opera House and Circular Quay

The iconic **Sydney Opera House** offers one of the most famous views in the world. While you're at the Opera House, you can take in the views of **Sydney Harbour** and the **Harbour Bridge**, with the stunning backdrop of the city skyline.

Best View: The view from the steps of the Opera House is spectacular, with the **Harbour Bridge** on one side and the city skyline on the other.

Nearby Lookouts: The **Royal Botanic Garden**, located right next to the Opera House, offers a relaxed setting with great views of the harbour and nearby islands.

2. Sydney Harbour Bridge

The **Sydney Harbour Bridge** is another iconic landmark that offers amazing views of the city and the harbour. For those looking for a unique experience, you can climb to the top of the bridge for a truly unforgettable view of Sydney.

BridgeClimb: If you're up for an adventure, the **BridgeClimb** takes you to the top of the bridge, offering 360-degree panoramic views of the city, the Opera House, and the harbour. Prices range from **AUD 150-400** depending on the time of day and type of experience.

Pylon Lookout: If you prefer a less strenuous option, the **Pylon Lookout** offers incredible views for a much lower price. It's located at the base of the bridge and costs around **AUD 15** for entry. ## 3. Mrs Macquarie's Chair

Located in the **Royal Botanic Garden, Mrs Macquarie's Chair** is one of the most popular scenic lookouts in Sydney. From here, you get a stunning view of **Sydney Harbour**, the Opera House, and the Harbour Bridge.

Best Time to Visit: Sunset is the perfect time to visit this spot, as the changing light makes for incredible photo opportunities. You'll also see the sun setting behind the city skyline.

Free Admission: The lookout is free to access and offers a peaceful spot to enjoy the view.

4. Bondi to Coogee Coastal Walk

Sydney's **Bondi to Coogee Coastal Walk** is one of the most scenic walks in the city, stretching over 6 kilometers along the coastline. The walk offers a variety of stunning lookouts, with breathtaking views of the Pacific Ocean, cliffs, and beaches.

Top Lookouts: Key points along the walk include **Marks Park**, which offers a panoramic view of Bondi Beach, and the **Glebe Point**, which offers sweeping views of the coastline towards Coogee.

Duration: The walk takes about 2-3 hours to complete, but you can take your time and stop at several lookouts along the way.

5. The Gap, Watsons Bay

Located in the eastern suburbs of Sydney, **The Gap** is a dramatic cliff that overlooks the Pacific Ocean. It offers a sweeping view of the coastline, the harbour entrance, and even the city in the distance.

Best View: The view from **The Gap** is especially stunning during sunrise or sunset, when the colors in the sky reflect off the ocean.

How to Get There: You can easily reach **The Gap** by taking a bus or ferry to **Watsons Bay**, then walking to the cliffside lookout. It's a great spot for a picnic or simply to take in the beauty of the area.

6. Ku-ring-gai Chase National Park Lookouts

For those who enjoy hiking and nature, **Ku-ring-gai Chase National Park**, located just north of Sydney, offers some of the most beautiful scenic lookouts. The park is home to rugged landscapes, lush bushland, and panoramic views of the **Hawkesbury River**.

Best Lookouts: Popular lookouts in the park include **West Head Lookout**, which offers views of the **Hawkesbury River** and nearby beaches, and **Woolwich Lookout**, which provides views of the river and the city skyline in the distance.

Hiking Trails: There are several walking trails in the park, ranging from easy strolls to more challenging hikes. Some trails, such as the **Resolute Beach Walk**, lead to secluded beaches and provide stunning views along the way.

7. North Head Lookout

Located in **Manly**, just across the harbour from the city, **North Head Lookout** offers panoramic views of the city, **Sydney Harbour**, and the Pacific Ocean. It's a quieter spot compared to some of the other lookouts, making it a great place to relax and take in the scenery.

Best View: From here, you can see the whole of **Sydney Harbour**, with the **Harbour Bridge** and **Opera House** in the distance.

Getting There: You can reach North Head by taking a bus or ferry to **Manly**, then hiking or driving to the lookout point.

8. Blue Mountains Lookouts

While not technically within the Sydney city limits, the **Blue Mountains** are just a short drive from Sydney and offer some of the most spectacular scenic views in the region. The **Blue Mountains National Park** is famous for its dramatic cliffs, valleys, and eucalyptus forests.

Top Lookouts: Popular spots include **Echo Point**, where you can see the famous **Three Sisters** rock formation, and **Govetts Leap Lookout**, which offers breathtaking views of the **Grose Valley**.

How to Get There: You can take a scenic train or drive to the **Blue Mountains** from Sydney in around 1.5-2 hours.

9. Barangaroo Reserve

Located near **Darling Harbour**, **Barangaroo Reserve** offers beautiful views of **Sydney Harbour** and the nearby city skyline. This newly developed waterfront park is a great place to relax while taking in views of the harbour.

Best Time to Visit: The view is particularly stunning at sunset, when the city's lights reflect on the water.

Free Admission: The park is free to access and features walking paths, picnic areas, and plenty of greenery, making it perfect for a leisurely stroll or a relaxing afternoon.

10. Centennial Park Lookouts

Centennial Park is one of Sydney's largest and most beautiful parks, offering peaceful spots to enjoy nature and take in the city skyline in the distance. The park is home to a variety of walking trails, wildlife, and gardens.

Best View: From **Gordon's Bay Lookout**, you can see across the park's fields and ponds, and the **City of Sydney** skyline in the background.

Getting There: Centennial Park is easily accessible by public transport, with several bus stops and train stations nearby.

Conclusion

Sydney is full of breathtaking scenic views and lookouts, from iconic landmarks like the Opera House and Harbour Bridge to hidden gems in national parks and coastal walks. Whether you're looking for a panoramic view of the city, a tranquil spot to relax, or a dramatic cliffside vista, Sydney offers something for every traveler. Make sure to visit these incredible lookouts for unforgettable views of this beautiful city!

4.4 Sydney Harbour Cruises

One of the best ways to experience Sydney's stunning coastline and iconic landmarks is from the water. **Sydney Harbour Cruises** offer an unforgettable perspective of the city, allowing you to take in views of the **Sydney Opera House**, **Sydney Harbour Bridge**, and the **Royal Botanic Garden**, among other beautiful sites. Whether you're looking for a leisurely sightseeing cruise, a romantic dinner experience, or an adventurous ferry ride, there are plenty of options to suit all tastes and budgets.

Here's a breakdown of the best Sydney Harbour cruises:

1. Sydney Harbour Sightseeing Cruises

These cruises are ideal for first-time visitors who want to see all of Sydney's major waterfront landmarks in one go. You'll enjoy a guided commentary as you sail past the Opera House, the Harbour Bridge, and various islands, as well as some lesser-known but equally beautiful spots along the coast.

Duration: These cruises typically last between 1 to 2 hours.

Cost: Prices start at around **AUD 30–60** per person, depending on the operator and the duration of the tour.

Best Time to Go: The afternoon or evening is a great time to catch the golden hour and the city's skyline as the sun sets. Many cruises offer evening departures, which allow you to see the lights of the city after dark.

Where to Depart: Cruises depart from Circular Quay or Darling Harbour, both of which are central locations and easily accessible by public transport.

2. Dinner Cruises

For a more romantic or special experience, consider booking a **dinner cruise** on Sydney Harbour. These cruises offer a more luxurious experience, combining fine dining with spectacular views. Enjoy a delicious meal while sailing past iconic landmarks and taking in the sights of the harbour as the sun sets.

Duration: Typically 2 to 3 hours.

Cost: Prices start from **AUD 100–200** per person, depending on the package, type of meal, and boat.

Menu: Most dinner cruises offer a buffet or à la carte dining, with options ranging from seafood and steak to vegetarian and vegan choices.

Best Experience: Enjoying a champagne while watching the sunset over the Harbour Bridge and Opera House is a highlight for many.

3. Luxury Cruises and Private Charters

If you're looking for a more exclusive experience, a luxury cruise or private charter is an excellent choice. These cruises offer premium amenities, personalized service, and an intimate atmosphere. You can charter a private boat for a more tailored experience, whether it's for a special occasion, corporate event, or simply a lavish day out.

Duration: Customizable, usually between 2–4 hours.

Cost: Luxury cruises typically start at around **AUD 500–1000** for a private boat, depending on the size of the vessel and the level of service.

Features: Some luxury cruises feature onboard gourmet meals, and even a personal guide. Private charters can include additional features like a private chef, music, and onboard entertainment.

Where to Depart: These cruises depart from Circular Quay or other private docks around the city.

4. Ferry Cruises

If you're on a budget but still want to experience the beauty of Sydney Harbour, hop on a **Sydney Ferry**. The ferry network is extensive, and several routes pass through the harbour, providing wonderful views of the waterfront. While ferries don't typically offer guided commentary or special amenities, they still provide an excellent way to explore Sydney by water.

Routes: The **Manly Ferry** is particularly popular, offering a scenic ride from Circular Quay to **Manly**, with views of the Opera House, Harbour Bridge, and the northern beaches. The **Neutral Bay** and **Taronga Zoo** ferries also offer great views.

Duration: The **Manly Ferry** ride takes about 30 minutes one way, but longer routes may take around 1 hour.

Cost: A one-way ferry ride costs between **AUD 7-10** depending on the route. If you're using an **Opal Card** (the public transport card), the fare will be discounted.

5. Eco-Friendly and Sustainable Cruises

Sydney Harbour also offers a selection of **ecofriendly cruises** that focus on sustainability and minimizing environmental impact. These cruises are typically run on electric or hybrid-powered boats and aim to give you a quiet and peaceful experience on the water while promoting eco-tourism.

Features: The eco-cruise experience includes minimal engine noise, slower speeds for better wildlife spotting, and educational commentary about protecting the harbour's ecosystem.

Cost: Prices generally range from **AUD 40–80** per person.

Duration: Eco cruises typically last 1.5 to 2 hours.

6. Special Themed Cruises

For something more unique, Sydney offers a variety of themed cruises throughout the year. These could range from **New Year's Eve Fireworks Cruises**, which allow you to watch the world-famous fireworks display from the water, **live music cruises**, and **holidaythemed cruises**.

Duration: Typically 2 to 3 hours, depending on the event.

Cost: Prices for themed cruises range from **AUD 50–150** per person, depending on the theme and time of year.

Best Time to Go: Themed cruises like the New Year's Eve cruise are very popular and sell out quickly, so it's important to book in advance.

7. Highlights of Sydney Harbour Cruises

Sydney Opera House: Sail past this world-renowned building and enjoy a close-up view from the water.

Sydney Harbour Bridge: Get a new perspective of the Harbour Bridge as you cruise under it.

Watson's Bay and The Gap: These dramatic cliffs and beaches are among Sydney's most scenic spots.

Cockatoo Island: One of Sydney's UNESCO World Heritage sites, offering great views and rich history.

Luna Park: The old-fashioned amusement park on the harbour, seen from the water.

Conclusion

Sydney Harbour cruises are an amazing way to explore the city from a unique perspective. Whether you're looking for a leisurely sightseeing cruise, an intimate dinner experience, or a budget-friendly ferry ride, there's a cruise to suit every traveler. From the stunning views of the Opera House and Harbour Bridge to the peaceful spots on the water, Sydney Harbour offers endless opportunities for adventure and relaxation. Be sure to book your cruise in advance, especially during peak tourist seasons, as they can fill up quickly!

4.5 Whale Watching

Sydney offers one of the best whale-watching experiences in the world. From **May to November**, humpback and southern right whales migrate along the Australian coast, and Sydney's waters are a prime location to spot these magnificent creatures. Whale watching tours provide an unforgettable opportunity to see these giants up close as they journey north and south along the coastline.

Best Time for Whale Watching

Season: The whale-watching season in Sydney runs from **May to November**.

> **May to August**: Whales are migrating north, heading to warmer waters for breeding.

September to November: Whales are migrating south after giving birth, heading back to Antarctic waters.

Best Months: The peak months for whale sightings are **June to August** when the whales are most active and numerous in the region.

Where to Go Whale Watching in Sydney

Sydney Harbour

Departure Point: Cruises often depart from **Circular Quay** or **Darling Harbour**.

What You'll See: While whale sightings in the harbour itself are rare, many tours offer a scenic journey out of the harbour and into the open ocean, where whales are often spotted.

Coastal Headlands

Bondi Beach: If you prefer to watch from land, **Bondi Beach** is a popular spot to see whales passing along the coast.

South Head: Located near **Watson's Bay**, South Head offers dramatic cliffs and panoramic ocean views, making it a great place to spot whales from shore.

Cape Solander: Situated in **Kurnell**, Cape Solander is a top whale-watching location with excellent vantage points along the cliffs.

North Head: Located in **Manly**, North Head offers stunning views of the Pacific Ocean and is another excellent location for spotting whales.

Types of Whale Watching Tours

Boat Tours

Duration: These tours typically last between **3 to 4 hours**, depending on the tour operator and the distance traveled.

Cost: Whale-watching cruises generally cost between **AUD 70–150** per person. Prices may vary depending on the type of boat, the duration, and the operator.

Departure Locations: Most tours depart from Circular Quay, Darling Harbour, or Manly. Boats take you out to open waters for the best chance to see the whales.

What's Included: Most whale-watching cruises offer a guide with live commentary, explaining whale behavior, migration patterns, and fun facts. Many boats also provide comfortable seating and refreshments.

Luxury Tours

For those looking for a more exclusive experience, **luxury whale-watching tours** offer premium amenities such as a more comfortable boat, gourmet meals, and private guides.

Duration: Typically 3–4 hours.

Cost: Prices for luxury tours usually start around **AUD 200–400** per person, depending on the package.

Kayak or Paddleboard Tours

For the adventurous, **kayak or paddleboard tours** offer an up-close experience of the ocean. These tours typically take place in more sheltered waters, like **Manly Cove**, and offer the thrill of being on the water with a chance to see dolphins, turtles, and even whales close up.

Duration: These tours last around 2 hours.

Cost: Prices range from **AUD 50–100** per person.

What to Expect on a Whale Watching Tour

Whale Sightings: The main highlight is, of course, spotting the whales. While no tour can guarantee sightings, Sydney's coastal waters are known for frequent encounters. You may witness spectacular displays, such as whales breaching (jumping out of the water), tail slapping, and spouting water from their blowholes.

Dolphins and Other Wildlife: Aside from whales, you may also see **dolphins**, **seals**, **sea birds**, and occasionally even **minke whales**. The waters around Sydney are rich in marine life.

Comfort: Modern whale-watching boats are equipped with amenities like comfortable seating, shaded areas, and onboard refreshments. Some boats even offer **underwater viewing rooms** for a unique experience of the whales up close.

Guides and Commentary: Expect knowledgeable guides to provide educational commentary about the species you encounter, their migration routes, and the environmental efforts to protect these majestic animals.

Tips for Whale Watching in Sydney

Book in Advance: Whale-watching tours can be very popular, especially during peak months (June–August), so it's a good idea to book your tour in advance.

Bring Layers: It can get chilly out on the water, so bring a jacket or sweater, even on sunny days.

Check the Weather: Whale watching is best done on clear, calm days. If the weather is rough or visibility is low, tours may be canceled or rescheduled.

Don't Forget Your Camera: Whale sightings are exciting and often fleeting, so having a camera or smartphone ready is a good idea. If you're hoping to capture high-quality photos, a zoom lens can be useful.

Be Patient: Whales are wild animals, and sightings aren't guaranteed. However, even if you don't spot a whale, the experience of being on the water, enjoying the scenic beauty, and spotting other marine life makes it worthwhile.

Conclusion

Whale watching in Sydney is a must-do activity for nature lovers and anyone visiting the city between May and November. Whether you're cruising the open waters or observing from the cliffs, Sydney offers some of the best whale-watching experiences in the world. Don't forget your camera, keep an eye out for these majestic creatures, and enjoy the stunning beauty of Sydney's coastline.

5. Sydney's Culture and Heritage

5.1 Aboriginal History and Cultural Significance

Sydney's history dates back tens of thousands of years, with its roots deeply embedded in the culture and traditions of its **Aboriginal peoples**. Before the arrival of European settlers, the area was home to several Aboriginal groups, the most prominent being the **Eora Nation**, the traditional custodians of the land around Sydney Harbour.

Aboriginal Connection to the Land

The **Eora people** inhabited the Sydney region for at least 50,000 years, living in harmony with the land and sea. Their culture is one of the oldest continuous cultures on Earth. The land, water, and animals were integral to their way of life, providing food, shelter, and spiritual significance. They had a deep connection to the environment, with sacred sites, ancestral lands, and natural landmarks forming part of their cultural identity.

The **Eora** are known for their intricate knowledge of the land, the seas, and the animals that inhabit the region. This relationship to the environment is captured in their stories, songs, and ceremonies, which have been passed down through generations.

Significance of Sydney Harbour

Sydney Harbour, with its iconic landscapes of cliffs, beaches, and islands, holds great cultural and spiritual importance to the Aboriginal people. For the **Eora**, the harbour was not just a source of food and water but also a place of connection to the Dreaming—an Aboriginal concept that ties the past, present, and future together through stories and ancestral beings.

The Rocks: This area, now a historic precinct in Sydney, was once an important site for the **Cadigal people**, a subgroup of the Eora Nation. The rocks and surrounding lands were places for trade, ceremonies, and social gatherings.

Circular Quay: Before the arrival of Europeans, **Circular Quay** (then known as **Warrane**) was a site of major cultural significance, with the Cadigal people using the area for fishing and socializing. Today, it continues to be a point of interest, especially given its historical connection to the first interactions between Aboriginal Australians and the British settlers.

Dreamtime and Aboriginal Spirituality

The Aboriginal culture is deeply influenced by the **Dreamtime**, the foundation of Aboriginal spiritual beliefs. Dreamtime refers to the time of creation when ancestral spirits formed the land, animals, and people. Each natural feature in Sydney's landscape—whether it's a rock, a tree, or a waterway—has a story tied to the Dreaming.

For example, **Bennelong Point**, where the Sydney Opera House stands today, is a significant location for the **Eora people** and named after **Bennelong**, a prominent Aboriginal man who was an intermediary between the Aboriginal people and the British settlers in the early days of European colonization.

Kangaroo Point and **Mosman** are areas associated with stories of the Dreamtime, where ancestral beings shaped the land and imparted knowledge to the people.

Aboriginal Art and Storytelling

Aboriginal art is one of the oldest forms of artistic expression in the world. Sydney is home to various exhibitions and galleries that showcase Aboriginal art, including the **Art Gallery of New South Wales** and the **Australian Museum**.

Aboriginal art is rich in symbolism and often tells the stories of the land, the animals, and the Dreaming. The artwork can be painted on bark, canvas, or rocks, and it may also appear in ceremonies, sculptures, and body art.

The **rock engravings** found around Sydney Harbour and the surrounding areas offer a glimpse into the cultural significance of the land. These engravings, depicting animals, footprints, and other spiritual symbols, are a form of storytelling passed down through generations.

Aboriginal Tours and Cultural Experiences

For visitors wishing to learn more about the Aboriginal history and culture of Sydney, there are several cultural tours and experiences available:

Aboriginal Guided Tours:

> **The Rocks Aboriginal Dreaming Tour**: This tour offers insight into the history and traditions of the **Eora people** and their connection to the land. It explores **The Rocks** area and features discussions on Aboriginal spirituality, history, and art.
>
> **Bondi to Coogee Coastal Walk**: A guided coastal walk with an Aboriginal guide where visitors can learn about the Aboriginal connection to the land and the sea, as well as the flora and fauna used by the indigenous people.

Cultural Centres and Galleries:

The Australian Museum: Offers exhibitions that celebrate Aboriginal cultures, history, and art. It features collections of Indigenous Australian artifacts, including tools, artworks, and photographs that give context to the ancient cultures of the land.

Bunjilaka Aboriginal Cultural Centre: Located at the Melbourne Museum, though not in Sydney, this center offers valuable insights into the broader Aboriginal culture and its significance.

Aboriginal Cultural Festivals:

NAIDOC Week: Celebrated across Australia, this week-long event honors the history, culture, and achievements of Aboriginal and Torres Strait Islander peoples. In Sydney, various events and activities are held, such as performances, storytelling, and art exhibitions.

Reconciliation Week: This week highlights the ongoing journey toward reconciliation between Aboriginal and non-Aboriginal Australians. There are usually community gatherings, cultural activities, and public events to raise awareness about Indigenous issues.

Contemporary Aboriginal Culture

Aboriginal culture is not just ancient history but is alive and evolving today. Many Aboriginal Australians continue to celebrate and share their culture through music, dance, art, and activism. Sydney is home to a growing number of Aboriginal artists, performers, and writers who contribute to the broader cultural landscape.

Aboriginal music and dance are an important part of Sydney's cultural scene, with performances held in galleries, festivals, and public spaces.

Aboriginal food and storytelling events are also becoming more popular, offering a chance for visitors to experience traditional bush foods and listen to elders share their stories.

Conclusion

Sydney's Aboriginal heritage is a central part of the city's identity, and understanding its history and significance adds depth to your experience when visiting the city. From the sacred sites around Sydney Harbour to the rich cultural expressions in art and performances, the Aboriginal culture provides a profound connection to the land and its people. Visitors who take the time to learn about Sydney's Indigenous history will gain a deeper appreciation of the city's past and present.

5.2 The Role of Sydney in Australia's History

Sydney is not just a vibrant, modern metropolis; it also plays a significant role in the history and development of Australia as a nation. From its early days as a British penal colony to becoming Australia's largest city and cultural capital, Sydney's history is deeply intertwined with the evolution of the country. Let's explore the key milestones in Sydney's history and its role in shaping Australia.

The Arrival of Europeans: 1788 and the First Fleet

Sydney's history as a European settlement began on **January 26, 1788**, when **Captain Arthur Phillip**, leading the **First Fleet**, arrived in Botany Bay, on the southeastern coast of Australia. This event marked the beginning of European colonization of Australia. However, due to unsuitable conditions, the fleet moved a few days later to **Port Jackson**, where they established the settlement at **Sydney Cove**.

This settlement is now known as **Sydney**, and it became the first permanent British colony on the

Australian continent. The arrival of the First Fleet is often referred to as the beginning of **Australia's colonial history**, although it was also the start of profound changes for the **Aboriginal peoples** of the land.

Convict Transportation and Early Settlement

As a penal colony, the early years of Sydney were marked by hardship and survival. The British government transported convicts from overcrowded prisons to the new colony in order to alleviate the pressure on the criminal justice system in Britain.

Between **1788 and 1868**, over 80,000 convicts were sent to Australia, many of whom were sent to Sydney. While the conditions in the early years were harsh, with convicts forced to work on public infrastructure and agricultural projects, the city slowly began to develop. Sydney's economy grew through the use of convict labor, which helped to lay the foundation for the city's future expansion.

Growth and Expansion in the 19th Century

By the mid-1800s, Sydney had evolved from a small settlement to a burgeoning port city. The early colonial economy was largely based on **agriculture**, **timber**, and **whaling**, with goods being shipped in and out of the harbor.

The Gold Rush: The discovery of gold in **New South Wales** in the **1850s** significantly contributed to Sydney's growth. As people flooded into the city in search of wealth, Sydney became a hub for trade and commerce. The city saw a rise in immigration, which helped to establish its multicultural character.

Public Infrastructure: Throughout the 19th century, Sydney began developing its public infrastructure. The construction of **railways**, **roads**, and **buildings** transformed the city. The iconic **Sydney Town Hall** and **Queen Victoria Building**, which were constructed in the late 19th century, are examples of this period of growth and architectural development.

Federation and Becoming the Nation's Gateway

One of Sydney's most important historical milestones was **Australia's Federation** in **1901**, which brought the six British colonies together to form the **Commonwealth of Australia**. Sydney, as the capital of **New South Wales**, played a key role in this process, though the nation's capital was eventually established in **Canberra**.

However, Sydney's role as the country's largest city and economic powerhouse remained unchanged. The city continued to be a central hub for trade, politics, and culture, and it became the entry point for migrants coming to Australia.

The Sydney Harbour Bridge: A Symbol of National Unity

In **1932**, the **Sydney Harbour Bridge** was completed, forever changing the city's skyline. The bridge, affectionately known as the **Coathanger**, became a symbol of Sydney's ambition and resilience. The opening of the bridge connected the city's north and south shores, facilitating trade and transportation. It was not just an engineering marvel but also a symbol of Australia's modernization and national unity.

The Harbour Bridge's significance goes beyond its physical role in connecting parts of Sydney; it became a metaphor for the coming together of the different states and territories in Australia. Its construction during the Great Depression also showcased the country's determination to overcome economic hardship.

World War II and Sydney's Strategic Importance

During **World War II**, Sydney played an important role in Australia's defense. The city was a key location for the Allied forces, serving as a base for military operations in the Pacific. The **Royal Australian Navy** and the **Royal Australian Air Force** were stationed in Sydney, and the city's ports were crucial for the supply of resources and troops.

Sydney itself was not directly attacked but felt the effects of the war, with air raids in northern Australia and the risk of invasion looming large. The war further solidified Sydney's status as an important city in both a national and international context.

Post-War Immigration and Urban Development

Following World War II, Sydney experienced a wave of **immigration**, as people from Europe, Asia, and the Middle East sought a better life in Australia. This influx of immigrants led to significant changes in the city's demographics and helped establish Sydney as one of the world's most multicultural cities.

With increased immigration came rapid urbanization. Sydney expanded its suburbs, and iconic buildings like the **Sydney Opera House** and the **Royal Australian Navy** base at **Garden Island** were developed. The city also began to shift from an industrial economy to a service-based economy, with finance, technology, and tourism becoming key drivers of growth.

Sydney in Modern Australia

Today, Sydney is not just the largest city in Australia; it is also a **global cultural, economic, and financial center**. As the country's most populous city, it remains a major hub for commerce, international trade, and tourism.

Sydney's history is also integral to Australia's national identity. The **Sydney Opera House**, **Harbour Bridge**, and **Bondi Beach** are just some of the iconic landmarks that represent the nation's history, culture, and achievements. Sydney remains a vital part of Australia's story, from its beginnings as a convict settlement to its present-day status as a world-class city.

Conclusion

Sydney has played an integral role in the history of Australia, from its humble beginnings as a penal colony to becoming a bustling metropolis. The city's history is not just about the development of a single urban area but reflects the growth and transformation of the nation as a whole. Sydney continues to stand as a symbol of **Australia's evolution**—from colonial settlement to modern prosperity. Understanding Sydney's role in Australia's history provides a deeper appreciation of the city and its importance within both the national and global contexts.

5.3 Art Galleries and Museums

Sydney is a cultural hub, home to many world-class art galleries and museums that showcase the city's rich history, vibrant contemporary culture, and diverse art forms. Whether you are an art enthusiast or just someone looking to explore, Sydney offers a wide array of museums and galleries that provide fascinating insights into Australia's artistic and cultural heritage.

Art Galleries

Art Gallery of New South Wales (AGNSW) The **Art Gallery of New South Wales** is one of Australia's leading public galleries, and it's free to visit. Located in **The Domain**, the gallery offers an extensive collection of Australian, European, and Asian art, spanning centuries of artistic movements. You'll find works from iconic Australian artists such as **Tom Roberts**, **Margaret Preston**, and **Sidney Nolan**, alongside European masterpieces by artists like **Vincent van Gogh** and **Claude Monet**. The gallery also frequently hosts temporary exhibitions, showcasing contemporary art from both local and international artists.
Address: Art Gallery Rd, The Domain, Sydney
Hours: Daily, 10:00 AM to 5:00 PM

Museum of Contemporary Art Australia (MCA) The **Museum of Contemporary Art** is located at **Circular Quay**, offering stunning views of **Sydney Harbour**. This modern museum specializes in contemporary Australian and international art, focusing on innovation, experimentation, and diverse artistic practices. The museum frequently hosts immersive exhibitions, artist talks, and interactive workshops. Highlights include works by **Tracey Moffatt**, **Christian Thompson**, and **David Hockney**.
Address: 140 George St, The Rocks, Sydney **Hours:** Daily, 10:00 AM to 5:00 PM

Australian   Museum

Sydney's **Australian Museum** is the oldest museum in Australia, focusing on natural history and cultural exhibitions. With permanent collections that explore Australia's Indigenous cultures, along with extensive displays on the natural world—including fossils, minerals, and animals—the museum offers a comprehensive view of Australia's natural and cultural history. The museum's **Dinosaur Gallery** and **Indigenous Australia** exhibition are popular attractions.

Address: 1 William St, Sydney
Hours: Daily, 10:00 AM to 5:00 PM

The   Nicholson   Museum

Situated at the **University of Sydney**, the **Nicholson Museum** is Australia's largest collection of antiquities. The museum showcases an impressive range of artifacts from ancient **Egypt**, **Rome**, **Greece**, and **Mesopotamia**. The museum's **Egyptian Mummy** is one of its most famous exhibits.

Address: University of Sydney, Camperdown, Sydney
Hours: Monday to Friday, 10:00 AM to 4:00 PM

Cultural Museums

The   Powerhouse   Museum

The **Powerhouse Museum** explores the intersection of technology, design, and science. It offers exhibits on the history of transport, space exploration, and even fashion. Interactive displays and rotating exhibitions ensure that there's always something new to discover, making it an engaging experience for people of all ages. **Address:** 500 Harris St, Ultimo, Sydney **Hours:** Daily, 10:00 AM to 5:00 PM

The Australian National Maritime Museum
This museum is dedicated to Australia's maritime history, covering everything from the country's colonial past to modern naval engagements. The museum is located at **Darling Harbour** and features interactive exhibits, including the famous **HMB Endeavour Replica**, a ship similar to the one captained by **James Cook** on his voyage to Australia. **Address:** 2 Murray St, Darling Harbour, Sydney **Hours:** Daily, 9:30 AM to 5:00 PM

5.4 Festivals and Cultural Events

Sydney is a vibrant city with a year-round calendar of exciting festivals and cultural events that celebrate its diverse population and rich artistic traditions. These festivals highlight the city's love for art, music, food, and multiculturalism, and they provide visitors with an opportunity to experience Sydney's cultural heartbeat.

Sydney Festival (January)

The **Sydney Festival** is one of the city's biggest cultural events, taking place every January. This month-long celebration is filled with **art performances**, **theatre shows**, **dance performances**, **live music**, and **street performances**. The festival is known for its international flair, featuring artists and performers from around the globe, alongside local talent. Major venues include **Hyde Park**, the **Sydney Opera House**, and various theatres around the city. **Notable Events:** Performances at the **Sydney Opera House**, free outdoor performances at **Hyde Park**, **art installations**, and **dance shows**. **Dates:** January (Exact dates vary) **Ticket Information:** Various ticket prices depending on the event. Some performances are free.

Vivid Sydney (May-June)

Vivid Sydney is a spectacular **light, music, and ideas festival** that transforms the city into a glowing artistic wonderland. The **Sydney Opera House** and **Sydney Harbour Bridge** light up with colorful projections, and art installations are displayed across the city. There are also incredible performances and talks about **innovation**, **technology**, and **creativity**. This annual event attracts visitors from around the world who want to experience the intersection of art and technology in a vibrant urban setting.
Notable Events: Light installations along **Circular Quay**, **laser shows** on **Sydney Harbour**, **live music performances**, and **talks on innovation**.
Dates: Late May to mid-June

Ticket Information: Many light installations and outdoor performances are free, but some events and exhibits may require a ticket.

Sydney Gay and Lesbian Mardi Gras (FebruaryMarch)

One of the largest LGBTQ+ festivals in the world, the **Sydney Gay and Lesbian Mardi Gras** is a colorful and vibrant celebration of equality, love, and acceptance. The highlight of the festival is the **Mardi Gras Parade**, where thousands of people march through **Oxford Street** in elaborate costumes, celebrating the diversity of the LGBTQ+ community. The festival also includes parties, art exhibitions, and musical   performances.

Notable Events: Mardi Gras Parade, **Mardi Gras Party**, **art exhibitions**, and **LGBTQ+ film screenings**.

Dates: February-March (Exact dates vary) **Ticket Information:** Parade is free to watch, but parties and some events may require tickets.

Sydney Writers' Festival (May)

The **Sydney Writers' Festival** is one of Australia's most prestigious literary events, attracting authors, poets, and thinkers from around the world. The festival celebrates literature in all its forms, including fiction, poetry, memoirs, and more. Events range from author talks and book signings to writing workshops and panel discussions. This festival is a must-attend for anyone passionate about reading and writing. **Notable**

Events: Author talks, **panel discussions**, **writing workshops**, and **book signings**.
Dates: May (Exact dates vary)
Ticket Information: Varies by event, but many events are free or low-cost.

Chinese New Year (January-February)

Sydney's **Chinese New Year** celebrations are one of the largest in the world, attracting hundreds of thousands of visitors. The festival celebrates the lunar calendar and features a **colorful parade**, **lion dances**, **traditional performances**, and **delicious food stalls**. The festivities extend across the city, with special events at **Chinatown**, **Darling Harbour**, and **Circular Quay**.
Notable Events: Lunar New Year Parade, **lion dances**, **street food markets**, and **cultural performances**.
Dates: January-February (Exact dates vary) **Ticket Information:** Most events are free.

Sydney's festivals and cultural events offer a unique opportunity to immerse yourself in the city's diverse and dynamic artistic scene. Whether you're into theater, visual arts, literature, or celebrations of cultural traditions, Sydney provides something for everyone to enjoy throughout the year.

6. Food and Drink in Sydney

6.1 Sydney's Culinary Scene

Sydney's food scene is as vibrant and diverse as the city itself, drawing inspiration from its multicultural population, coastal lifestyle, and local produce. From fresh seafood and fine dining to street food markets and fusion restaurants, Sydney offers a wide range of dining experiences that are sure to satisfy every taste and budget.

Fresh Seafood

Sydney's position along the coast means that fresh seafood is a major feature of its culinary offerings. The **Sydney Fish Market**, located in **Pyrmont**, is one of the largest seafood markets in the Southern Hemisphere and an absolute must-visit for seafood lovers. Here, you can find a variety of fresh fish, shellfish, and crustaceans, including **Sydney rock oysters**, **mud crabs**, **prawns**, and **lobsters**. The market also has restaurants and food stalls where you can enjoy seafood dishes straight from the source.

For a more upscale seafood experience, the **Sydney Opera House** houses **Bennelong**, a fine-dining restaurant that serves Australian seafood with a modern twist, offering a unique dining experience with breathtaking views of **Sydney Harbour**.

Fusion and Multicultural Influences

Sydney's food scene reflects its diverse population, with restaurants serving food from all over the world. **Asian cuisine** plays a significant role, with many establishments specializing in Chinese, Thai, Japanese, Vietnamese, and Korean dishes. The **Chinatown** area is home to a wide variety of Asian restaurants, from dumpling houses to noodle shops and vibrant street food vendors.

For a fusion twist, many modern Australian restaurants offer creative takes on traditional recipes, blending Asian, Mediterranean, and European flavors. **Chin Chin**, located in **Surry Hills**, is an excellent example of a fusion restaurant, serving vibrant dishes like **Thai-style pork belly** and **sriracha fried rice** in a stylish, relaxed setting.

Modern Australian Cuisine

Modern Australian cuisine, or **"Mod Oz"**, is an exciting and ever-evolving genre of food that combines native ingredients with international influences. This type of cuisine often includes uniquely Australian ingredients like **wattleseed**, **finger lime**, and **bush tomatoes**, paired with global cooking techniques and flavors.

Restaurants like **Quay** (located in **The Rocks**) and **Aria** (at **Circular Quay**) are some of the city's most famous fine-dining venues offering modern Australian cuisine. These restaurants focus on creating innovative dishes using local ingredients, often with an emphasis on sustainability and seasonality.

Café Culture and Brunch Spots

Sydney is famous for its **café culture**, with countless cafés offering delicious breakfast and brunch options. **Coffee culture** is a big part of life here, and you'll find some of the best coffee in the world, with many cafés sourcing beans from local roasters. Whether you're after a strong **flat white** or a light **cappuccino**, Sydney has countless cafés to suit every taste.

Popular brunch spots like **Bills** (in **Surry Hills**) and **The Grounds of Alexandria** are staples for locals and visitors alike. Dishes like **ricotta hotcakes**, **avocado toast**, and **eggs benedict** are menu highlights that pair perfectly with a cup of expertly brewed coffee.

Street Food and Markets

Sydney is home to vibrant street food markets that serve up an array of international flavors at affordable prices. **Paddys Markets** (in **Haymarket**) is a bustling spot offering a range of street food, including dumplings, bánh mì sandwiches, and other Asianinspired dishes. **Glebe Markets** is another popular weekend market where you can sample fresh, locally sourced food from food trucks and stalls serving everything from tacos to vegan burgers.

Carriageworks Farmers Market, located in **Eveleigh**, is one of the best places to experience Sydney's focus on fresh, sustainable produce. Open every Saturday, it's a hub for local farmers, artisans, and food producers selling everything from organic fruits and vegetables to freshly baked goods, cheeses, and cured meats.

Iconic Sydney Foods

Sydney has a number of iconic foods that you shouldn't miss during your visit:

Meat Pies: An Australian classic, the humble meat pie is a favorite quick meal or snack. Filled with meat, gravy, and sometimes vegetables, these pies are sold everywhere from bakeries to convenience stores. The **Harry's Café de Wheels** in **Woolloomooloo** is famous for its pies and is a great spot to try this Australian favorite.

Tim Tams: This iconic Australian biscuit (cookie) is a chocolate-covered treat filled with chocolate cream. You'll find Tim Tams at almost every supermarket, and it's a must-try snack during your stay.

Lamingtons: A spongy cake covered in chocolate and rolled in coconut, **Lamingtons** are a beloved dessert in Australia. Many bakeries and cafés serve them, and they're a great snack to accompany your afternoon coffee.

Vegemite: A uniquely Australian spread made from yeast extract, **Vegemite** is often spread on toast and enjoyed with butter. It's an acquired taste, but it's definitely something to try during your trip!

Fine Dining Experiences

For those looking to indulge in a high-end dining experience, Sydney offers several Michelin-starred and award-winning restaurants. As mentioned earlier, **Quay** and **Aria** are top contenders. But there are other notable places like **Tetsuya's**, where Japanese influences blend with modern Australian flavors, and **Bennelong**, where contemporary Australian cuisine is enjoyed in one of Sydney's most iconic locations.

Sydney is also home to many **rooftop bars and restaurants** where you can dine with a view of the stunning city skyline. **Sky Terrace**, located atop the **Sydney Tower**, offers a full dining experience with panoramic views.

Sustainable and Local Eating

Sydney has a growing interest in sustainable and farmto-table dining, with many restaurants and cafés committed to reducing food waste and supporting local farmers. Many eateries, including **Vino e Cucina** in **Surry Hills**, focus on **organic** and **locally grown** produce, ensuring fresh and sustainable ingredients are used in every dish. If you're keen on exploring sustainability in Sydney's culinary scene, consider visiting the **Earth Markets** or joining **food tours** that focus on local and organic produce.

Final Thoughts

Sydney's culinary scene is diverse, innovative, and full of delicious options for every budget. From fresh seafood and multicultural dishes to high-end fine dining and bustling food markets, there's something to suit every taste. Whether you're indulging in a luxurious meal overlooking **Sydney Harbour**, or grabbing a quick bite from a street food vendor, Sydney offers an unforgettable gastronomic adventure.

6.2 Seafood and Famous Fish Markets

Sydney's coastal location makes it one of the best places in the world to experience fresh seafood. The city boasts some of the finest seafood restaurants and seafood markets, where you can enjoy a wide variety of fresh catches from the ocean. Whether you prefer fish, shellfish, or something more exotic, Sydney has it all, and there's no better place to start your seafood adventure than at the famous **Sydney Fish Market**.

Sydney Fish Market

Located in **Pyrmont**, the **Sydney Fish Market** is a bustling, vibrant hub for seafood lovers. It's one of the largest seafood markets in the Southern Hemisphere, with more than 100 different species of seafood sold daily. The market opens early, typically around **5:00 AM** for wholesalers, and stays open to the public until **4:00 PM**. It's the place to go for the freshest seafood in Sydney.

What to Expect at the Sydney Fish Market:

Variety: You'll find everything from **Sydney rock oysters** to **mud crabs**, **lobsters**, **prawns**, **salmon**, and **tuna**. There are also specialty seafood items like **scallops**, **octopus**, and **abalone**. The variety is incredible, and you can get a real taste of Australia's finest catch.

Seafood Auctions: One of the unique features of the Sydney Fish Market is the daily seafood auction, where wholesalers bid on the day's freshest catches. Visitors can watch the action, and if you're lucky, you might even be able to purchase some of the catch directly from the market.

Seafood Restaurants and Food Stalls: The market isn't just a place to buy seafood; it's also a great spot to enjoy some fresh dishes. There are several restaurants and takeaway stalls inside the market serving everything from **fish and chips** to **sushi**, **oysters on the half shell**, and **grilled prawns**. **Doyles on the Wharf**, a long-established seafood restaurant at the market, is a must-visit for anyone looking to indulge in a premium seafood meal with a view of the harbor.

Address and Contact Information:

Sydney Fish Market

Location: **Pyrmont Bridge Road, Pyrmont, NSW 2009**

Phone: **+61 2 9004 1100**

Website: www.sydneyfishmarket.com.au

Where to Enjoy Seafood in Sydney

Beyond the Fish Market, there are plenty of other places in Sydney where you can enjoy fresh seafood, from high-end restaurants to laid-back eateries by the beach.

Bennelong: Located in the **Sydney Opera House**, **Bennelong** is one of Sydney's premier fine dining establishments, offering a menu centered on Australian seafood. Signature dishes include **Tasmanian salmon** and **blue swimmer crab**.

The Boathouse Palm Beach: Situated by the water at **Palm Beach**, this popular spot is perfect for a relaxed seafood experience, offering seafood platters, fresh oysters, and grilled fish with views over the water.

Sydney Cove Oyster Bar: Right next to **Circular Quay**, this casual yet sophisticated spot specializes in fresh oysters, served with a selection of condiments. You can also enjoy other seafood dishes like **fish tacos** or **prawn cocktails**.

The Bucket List Bondi: For those who prefer a beachside dining experience, **The Bucket List** in **Bondi** offers a laid-back atmosphere and a delicious selection of fresh seafood. From **lobster rolls** to **fish and chips**, it's a great spot for enjoying Sydney's famous seafood right on the beach.

Popular Sydney Seafood Dishes to Try

Sydney offers many famous seafood dishes that you should definitely try while visiting the city:

Fish and Chips: A classic Aussie meal, often served with **battered flathead** or **whiting** alongside crispy fries and a side of tartar sauce. You can find this dish at almost every seafood restaurant and takeaway stall in Sydney.

Oysters: Sydney's **Sydney rock oysters** are considered some of the best in the world. Fresh and briny, these oysters are often served with a squeeze of lemon or a dash of vinegar and shallots. You can enjoy them at restaurants like **Sydney Cove Oyster Bar** or buy them fresh at the **Sydney Fish Market**.

Prawns: Known for their sweetness and tenderness, **Sydney prawns** are a must-try. Whether grilled, served in a curry, or enjoyed in a **seafood cocktail**, they are a Sydney favorite.

Mud Crabs: Found in the waters off **Queensland** and northern **New South Wales**, mud crabs are a popular dish in Sydney. They are often steamed or stirfried with garlic, ginger, and chili for a flavorful, spicy dish.

Prawn and Scallop Mornay: A decadent dish often served at high-end seafood restaurants, featuring prawns and scallops in a creamy cheese sauce.

Sustainable Seafood in Sydney

Sustainability is becoming an increasingly important factor when choosing seafood. Many of Sydney's restaurants and fish markets focus on offering sustainable options that are responsibly sourced. The **Sydney Fish Market** has a dedicated **Sustainable Seafood Program**, which works with suppliers to ensure that seafood sold at the market is caught using environmentally friendly methods.

When dining out, it's a good idea to look for restaurants that highlight their commitment to sustainable seafood practices, such as **Fish4Ever** and **Sustainable Seafood Australia**. By supporting these restaurants and markets, you can enjoy delicious seafood while contributing to the protection of marine ecosystems.

Final Thoughts

Sydney's seafood offerings are diverse, fresh, and delicious, with something to satisfy every seafood lover. Whether you're shopping at the **Sydney Fish Market** for fresh prawns, enjoying a gourmet meal at a top restaurant, or grabbing a casual bite by the beach, Sydney's seafood scene is an essential part of the city's culinary culture. Make sure to explore the variety of dishes and flavors available, and enjoy one of the best seafood experiences in the world.

6.3 Dining in Darling Harbour and Circular Quay

Sydney's **Darling Harbour** and **Circular Quay** are two of the city's most iconic waterfront areas, offering a wide range of dining experiences. From casual cafes with scenic views to fine dining restaurants with worldclass cuisine, both locations provide exceptional places to eat and drink. Here's a comprehensive guide to dining in these two vibrant precincts.

Darling Harbour Dining

Darling Harbour is a bustling entertainment and dining district in the heart of Sydney. With a beautiful waterfront setting, it's a perfect place to enjoy a meal while taking in views of the harbor. The area is home to a mix of restaurants, cafes, and food courts, serving everything from international dishes to Australian classics.

Key Dining Spots in Darling Harbour:

The   Watershed
If you're looking for a casual yet refined spot with views over the harbor, **The Watershed** is a great option. It offers a modern Australian menu with an emphasis on fresh local produce. Try their **grilled barramundi** or **Australian steaks**.

Address: **Cockle Bay Wharf, Darling Harbour**

Price Range: $20-$45 per main dish

Contact: +61 2 9283 1988

Hurricane's   Grill   Darling   Harbour
For those craving some hearty **ribs** and **steaks**, **Hurricane's Grill** at Darling Harbour is the place to be. Famous for its **succulent baby back ribs**, **grilled meats**, and **seafood platters**, this lively restaurant is ideal for groups and families.

Address: Shop 15/16, Darling Harbour

Price Range: $30-$60 per main dish

Contact: +61 2 9283 3651

Mr. **Wong**
Mr. Wong brings upscale Cantonese dining to Darling Harbour. It's part of the **Merivale Group**, known for its trendy and stylish restaurants. Mr. Wong is perfect for a special night out, offering a range of dishes like **dim sum**, **crispy duck**, and **barbecued pork**.

Address: 11 Bridge Lane, Darling Harbour

Price Range: $30-$80 per main dish

Contact: +61 2 9240 3000

Pancakes **on** **the** **Rocks**
For a more laid-back experience, **Pancakes on the Rocks** serves classic American-style pancakes alongside burgers, steaks, and seafood. It's a great family-friendly spot, especially for dessert lovers who can indulge in giant, sweet pancakes and milkshakes.

Address: Harbourside Shopping Centre, Darling Harbour

Price Range: $15-$30 per dish

Contact: +61 2 9264 3193

Wild Life Sydney Zoo Café
Situated near the **Wild Life Sydney Zoo**, this café offers a perfect spot for families to grab a quick bite after exploring the zoo. The café serves simple, kidfriendly meals such as sandwiches, pastries, and healthy snacks, all with a view of Darling Harbour.

Address: 1-5 Wheat Road, Darling Harbour

Price Range: $10-$25 per dish

Contact: +61 2 9333 9288

Circular Quay Dining

Circular Quay is Sydney's transport hub, offering a picturesque location with views of the **Sydney Opera House** and **Sydney Harbour Bridge**. It's also a fantastic dining destination, with restaurants that range from casual eateries to more sophisticated dining options. Circular Quay provides an ideal mix of fine dining, classic Australian dishes, and international flavors.

Key Dining Spots in Circular Quay:

Quay Restaurant
For an unforgettable fine dining experience, **Quay** is one of the most renowned restaurants in Sydney. Located in the **Overseas Passenger Terminal**, it offers a contemporary Australian menu with stunning views of the Opera House and Harbour Bridge. **Chef**

Peter Gilmore creates a multi-course tasting menu using the finest seasonal ingredients.

Address: **Overseas Passenger Terminal, Circular Quay**

Price Range: $175-$300 for tasting menu

Contact: +61 2 9251 5600

Aria   Restaurant

Situated just across from the Opera House, **Aria** offers exquisite views of Sydney Harbour paired with modern Australian cuisine. With a focus on fresh, local ingredients, the menu features beautifully prepared dishes such as **seared scallops** and **slow-cooked lamb shoulder**. It's a top choice for special occasions.

Address: **1 Macquarie Street, Circular Quay**

Price Range: $40-$100 per main dish

Contact: +61 2 9240 2255

Café   Sydney

With one of the best views in Sydney, **Café Sydney** is perched on top of the **Customs House** at Circular Quay. Offering fresh Australian produce and seafood, the restaurant serves signature dishes like **Sydney rock oysters** and **grilled barramundi**. The outdoor seating area is perfect for enjoying the harbor views.

Address: 31 Alfred Street, Circular Quay

Price Range: $30-$60 per main dish

Contact: +61 2 9251 8683

Opera Bar

If you're looking for a casual yet iconic dining experience, **Opera Bar** is a must-visit. Located right next to the **Sydney Opera House**, it offers a wide range of snacks, drinks, and meals, from fresh seafood to pizzas and burgers. It's the perfect place to enjoy a drink while taking in views of the Opera House and the Harbour Bridge.

Address: Bennelong Point, Circular Quay

Price Range: $15-$40 per dish

Contact: +61 2 9247 4662

The Dining Room at Park Hyatt

The **Park Hyatt Hotel** offers a luxurious dining experience at **The Dining Room**, with panoramic views of the Harbour Bridge. The menu features modern Australian dishes with an emphasis on seafood, like **pan-seared lobster** and **grilled kingfish**. The elegant setting and outstanding service make it perfect for a special dining experience.

Address: 7 Hickson Road, Circular Quay

Price Range: $50-$100 per main dish

Contact: +61 2 9256 1611

Final Thoughts

Both **Darling Harbour** and **Circular Quay** are fantastic destinations for food lovers, offering a wide range of dining options from casual bites to fine dining experiences. Whether you're looking for fresh seafood, modern Australian cuisine, or international dishes, these areas have something to suit every taste and budget. Enjoy your meals with stunning views of the Sydney Harbour and iconic landmarks like the **Opera House** and **Harbour Bridge**.

6.4 Best Cafes and Brunch Spots in Sydney

Sydney is known for its vibrant café culture, with many spots offering delicious breakfast and brunch options, from classic Aussie fare to innovative global dishes. Whether you're a coffee aficionado, a fan of avocado toast, or someone who loves sweet pastries, Sydney has the perfect café to satisfy your cravings. Here's a guide to some of the best cafes and brunch spots across the city.

1. The Grounds of Alexandria

Located in the trendy suburb of Alexandria, **The Grounds of Alexandria** is a café and eatery that has become an institution in Sydney's brunch scene. Set within a sprawling space that includes a garden, a café, a bakery, and even a farm, this place offers a delightful, rustic ambiance perfect for enjoying a leisurely breakfast or brunch. They serve up freshly roasted coffee, artisanal pastries, and innovative brunch options like **breakfast burgers**, **acai bowls**, and **pancakes with caramelized bananas**.

Address: **7a/2 Huntley St, Alexandria**

Price Range: $15–$30 per person

Contact: +61 2 9699 2225

2. Single O

If you're a coffee enthusiast, **Single O** in Surry Hills is a must-visit. This café is known for its specialty coffee, brewed with beans that are sourced from some of the best coffee-growing regions. The café has an industrialchic feel, and its menu is full of mouthwatering brunch options such as **smashed avocado on sourdough**, **bacon and egg rolls**, and the crowd favorite, **matcha waffles**.

Address: **60-64 Reservoir St, Surry Hills**

Price Range: $15–$25 per person

Contact: +61 2 9211 0094

3. Reuben Hills

Located in Surry Hills, **Reuben Hills** offers a modern twist on traditional brunch options. Known for its specialty coffee, the café is also famous for its delicious **reuben sandwiches** and inventive dishes like **corn**

fritters with smoked salmon and **smashed pumpkin on toast**. The open-plan space gives off a relaxed vibe, and it's perfect for a lazy weekend brunch.

Address: 61-63 Albion St, Surry Hills

Price Range: $15–$30 per person

Contact: +61 2 9211 1215

4. Three Blue Ducks

Located in the hip suburb of Bronte, **Three Blue Ducks** is a café that emphasizes locally-sourced, organic ingredients. It's well-known for offering both traditional and innovative brunch options. Highlights include **crispy eggs with chorizo**, **shakshuka**, and **bacon butties**. If you're looking for a more healthconscious brunch, they also offer nutritious bowls and salads, such as the **grains and greens bowl**.

Address: 141-143 Macpherson St, Bronte

Price Range: $20–$40 per person

Contact: +61 2 9389 0010

5. Black Star Pastry

Famous for its **strawberry watermelon cake**, **Black Star Pastry** is an Instagram-worthy café that has become one of Sydney's most popular brunch spots. Located in Newtown, this café serves a variety of pastries, cakes, and savory items like **avocado toast with feta** and **smashed pumpkin on sourdough**. It's the perfect place to grab a sweet treat paired with a cup of artisan coffee.

Address: **277 Australia St, Newtown**

Price Range: $10–$25 per person

Contact: +61 2 9557 8656

---

6. Bills

A beloved Sydney institution, **Bills** is where you'll find some of the best breakfast dishes in town. Bills' famous **sweet corn fritters** and **ricotta hotcakes** are a must-try. Located in Darlinghurst, the café offers a cozy environment and a relaxed vibe perfect for those seeking a hearty, flavorful brunch. Don't forget to try their **Bills' eggs** served any style, along with their famous **banana bread**.

Address: **433 Liverpool St, Darlinghurst**

Price Range: $20–$35 per person

Contact: +61 2 9360 9631

7. Bread & Circus

For those who appreciate fresh, organic food, **Bread & Circus** in Alexandria is a great spot for a wholesome brunch experience. The café serves up delicious dishes with an emphasis on locally-sourced and sustainable ingredients. Try their **scrambled eggs with avocado**, **roasted mushroom toast**, or **coconut chia pudding**. The café also offers a range of fresh juices and smoothies to complement your meal.

Address: **21-23 Willoughby Rd, Alexandria**

Price Range: $15–$30 per person

Contact: +61 2 9690 2100

8. Café Sydney

Located on the rooftop of the **Customs House** at Circular Quay, **Café Sydney** is known for its stunning views of the Sydney Harbour and Opera House. While it's a bit more upscale, the café's brunch offerings are equally impressive. Enjoy classic brunch dishes like **eggs benedict**, **pancakes with maple syrup**, and **fresh seafood platters**, all while overlooking one of the best views in Sydney.

Address: **31 Alfred St, Circular Quay**

Price Range: $25–$45 per person

Contact: +61 2 9251 8683

9. The Apartment Café

Situated in the trendy suburb of Potts Point, **The Apartment Café** offers a cozy, homey atmosphere, perfect for a relaxing brunch. The menu features delicious options like **smashed avocado with feta**, **breakfast burritos**, and **sweet potato fritters**. This is a great spot for a casual, laid-back brunch with excellent coffee and freshly baked pastries.

Address: 3/73 Macleay St, Potts Point

Price Range: $15–$25 per person

Contact: +61 2 9331 2150

10. Gumption by Coffee Alchemy

Located in the **Surry Hills** area, **Gumption by Coffee Alchemy** is the go-to place for coffee lovers looking for an exceptional cup of coffee paired with a light brunch. While the focus is on high-quality coffee, their selection of pastries and simple brunch options, such as **toast with smashed avocado and poached eggs**, make it a perfect stop before heading out to explore the area.

Address: 3/72-74 Albion St, Surry Hills

Price Range: $10–$20 per person

Contact: +61 2 9211 8888

Final Thoughts

Sydney's café scene is a reflection of its diverse and vibrant culture, offering everything from trendy, Instagram-worthy spots to cozy, family-run cafés. Whether you're craving a healthy brunch, a decadent pastry, or a strong cup of coffee, you'll find a café that suits your taste in Sydney. Make sure to check out these top spots and enjoy some of the best brunch experiences the city has to offer!

7. Family-Friendly

Activities in Sydney

7.1 Best Family Attractions in Sydney

Sydney is an excellent destination for families, offering a wide range of activities that are fun, educational, and engaging for all ages. From world-famous wildlife parks to exciting interactive museums, here are some of the best family-friendly attractions in Sydney:

1. Taronga Zoo Sydney

One of the most iconic family attractions in Sydney, **Taronga Zoo** is home to over 4,000 animals from across the globe, including kangaroos, koalas, giraffes, and elephants. The zoo offers interactive experiences, such as animal encounters and behind-the-scenes tours, that allow kids to get up close to their favorite animals. The zoo also features breathtaking views of Sydney Harbour, making it a great spot for a family day out.

Location: **Bradleys Head Rd, Mosman**

Entry Price: Adults $49, Children (4-15 years) $29, Children under 4 years: Free

Contact: +61 2 9969 2777

2. SEA LIFE Sydney Aquarium

Located at **Darling Harbour**, **SEA LIFE Sydney Aquarium** is one of the largest aquariums in the world. The aquarium features a wide variety of marine life, including sharks, rays, turtles, and the famous dugongs. Kids can walk through glass tunnels that provide a 360-degree view of the aquatic animals swimming around them. The aquarium also offers interactive displays, such as touch pools and feeding demonstrations, to engage children in learning about marine ecosystems.

Location: **Aquarium Wharf, Darling Harbour**

Entry Price: Adults $47, Children (4-15 years) $30, Children under 4 years: Free

Contact: +61 2 9333 9288

3. Sydney Tower Eye

For families looking for an amazing view of Sydney, the **Sydney Tower Eye** is the place to go. At 309 meters tall, it is the highest point in the city, offering panoramic views of Sydney's skyline, harbor, and beyond. Kids will love the interactive displays at the tower, and for an extra thrill, families can try the **Skywalk**, an outdoor glass-floored walk around the tower.

Location: **100 Market St, Sydney**

Entry Price: Adults $32, Children (4-15 years) $22, Children under 4 years: Free

Contact: +61 2 9333 9222

4. Royal Botanic Garden

The **Royal Botanic Garden** offers a tranquil yet exciting experience for families, with vast green spaces for picnics, play, and exploration. Kids can enjoy running around, playing games, or discovering the many plants, flowers, and wildlife in the gardens. The garden also has a **Cranes Garden**, where children can learn about Australian wildlife through interactive displays and fun activities. The garden offers free guided tours and special children's programs throughout the year.

Location: **Mrs Macquaries Rd, Sydney**

Entry Price: Free

Contact: +61 2 9231 8111

5. Australian Museum

The **Australian Museum** is perfect for families interested in history, science, and natural wonders. The museum features interactive exhibits on dinosaurs, ancient cultures, Australian wildlife, and more. The **Wildlife Photographer of the Year** exhibition is particularly popular with younger visitors. The museum also offers educational workshops and programs for children to learn about science and nature in a fun and hands-on way.

Location: **1 William St, Darlinghurst**

Entry Price: Adults $15, Children (5-15 years) $7, Children under 5 years: Free

Contact: +61 2 9320 6000

6. Darling Harbour and Barangaroo Reserve

Darling Harbour is an ideal destination for families, with a variety of attractions including **Tumbalong Park**, where kids can enjoy playgrounds and water features. Right next door is **Barangaroo Reserve**, a beautiful park with sweeping views of the harbor. Kids can explore the park's walking trails, spot wildlife, and enjoy the outdoor spaces. There are also plenty of family-friendly restaurants in the area to grab a bite after a day of fun.

Location: **Darling Harbour, Sydney**

Entry Price: Free (individual attractions like playgrounds may have fees) **Contact**: +61 2 9240 8500

7. Wild Life Sydney Zoo

For families that want to experience Australia's native wildlife up close, **Wild Life Sydney Zoo** is a mustvisit. Located in **Darling Harbour**, the zoo features Australian animals like kangaroos, koalas, wombats, and crocodiles. The zoo offers a unique experience with interactive animal encounters, allowing kids to touch and learn about Australian wildlife in a safe and educational environment.

Location: **1-5 Wheat Rd, Darling Harbour**

Entry Price: Adults $42, Children (4-15 years) $28, Children under 4 years: Free

Contact: +61 2 9333 9288

8. Luna Park Sydney

Luna Park is a historic amusement park located in **Milsons Point** and is ideal for a fun family day. With a range of rides, including roller coasters, Ferris wheels, and spinning rides, the park offers entertainment for both younger kids and thrill-seekers. There are also carnival games, food stalls, and plenty of photo opportunities with the iconic **Luna Park Face**. **Location: 1 Olympic Dr, Milsons Point**

Entry Price: Free entry, Ride tickets: $10–$20 per ride

Contact: +61 2 9922 1640

9. Sydney Olympic Park

For families looking for outdoor activities, **Sydney Olympic Park** offers a wide range of recreational facilities. You can visit the **Parks** and **Playgrounds**, go cycling along the scenic pathways, or take part in organized sports activities. The **Aquatic Centre** is great for a family swim, and **Sydney Olympic Park** also hosts various events throughout the year that are ideal for children.

Location: Sydney Olympic Park, Homebush Bay

Entry Price: Free to access parks; individual attractions may have fees

Contact: +61 2 9704 1111

10. Sydney's Beaches (Family-Friendly)

Sydney's beaches are not only a great place for swimming but also perfect for family-friendly activities. **Bondi Beach** and **Coogee Beach** offer gentle waves for kids to enjoy. The coastal walks along these beaches provide scenic views and are a great way for families to explore Sydney's coastline together. Many of the beaches also have kid-friendly facilities, including playgrounds, shaded areas, and cafes.

Location: **Bondi Beach, Coogee Beach, and other Sydney beaches Entry Price**: Free

Contact: Varies by beach

Final Thoughts

Sydney is packed with family-friendly attractions that offer something for everyone, from animal encounters at the zoo to learning experiences at museums and outdoor fun on its beautiful beaches. Whether your kids are animal lovers, history buffs, or adventure seekers, Sydney has endless opportunities for family fun and bonding. Make sure to include these attractions in your itinerary to create lasting memories with your family!

2. Powerhouse Museum

The **Powerhouse Museum** is all about science, technology, and design, offering an interactive experience that will fascinate kids and adults alike. From space exploration to robotics and design, the museum's hands-on exhibits allow visitors to get involved and learn through play. Children can engage in interactive science experiments, test engineering designs, and even create their own inventions in the **MakerSpace**.

Location: 500 Harris St, Ultimo

Entry Price: Adults $15, Children (2-16 years) $10, Children under 2 years: Free

Contact: +61 2 9217 0111

Why Visit: The Powerhouse Museum's interactive exhibits make it an ideal stop for kids who love technology and problem-solving activities.

3. SEA LIFE Sydney Aquarium

SEA LIFE Sydney Aquarium offers a fun, educational experience for families, where kids can discover the underwater world of marine life through interactive touch pools and guided animal feedings.

Children can touch starfish, learn about marine conservation, and explore ocean habitats through interactive exhibits that feature sharks, turtles, and penguins. The aquarium's **Ocean Tunnel** provides a

360-degree view of the marine life swimming above and around visitors.

Location: Aquarium Wharf, Darling Harbour

Entry Price: Adults $47, Children (4-15 years) $30, Children under 4 years: Free

Contact: +61 2 9333 9288

Why Visit: SEA LIFE is perfect for families who want to interact with marine life and learn about ocean ecosystems. The hands-on exhibits allow children to learn while having fun.

4. Taronga Zoo Sydney

Taronga Zoo is not just a zoo – it's an interactive wildlife experience. The zoo features a wide range of exhibits, including the **Wild Ropes Adventure**, where families can participate in an exciting rope course through the treetops. Kids can also learn about animal conservation by participating in interactive programs and animal encounters, where they can get close to kangaroos, koalas, and even reptiles. The zoo's **Zoo Adventures** program also allows children to learn about different animal species and their habitats.

Location: Bradleys Head Rd, Mosman

Entry Price: Adults $49, Children (4-15 years) $29, Children under 4 years: Free

Contact: +61 2 9969 2777

Why Visit: Taronga Zoo provides an interactive experience with plenty of opportunities for families to engage with animals and learn about conservation.

---

5. Wild Life Sydney Zoo

Located in Darling Harbour, **Wild Life Sydney Zoo** offers an up-close look at Australia's unique animals. The zoo features an interactive **Koala Encounter** and offers opportunities to feed and learn about kangaroos, wombats, and other native wildlife. Children can take part in the **Wildlife Warrior program**, where they can learn about the different animals and their natural habitats through fun and educational experiences. **Location**: 1-5 Wheat Rd, Darling Harbour

Entry Price: Adults $42, Children (4-15 years) $28, Children under 4 years: Free

Contact: +61 2 9333 9288

Why Visit: Wild Life Sydney Zoo provides a hands-on experience with native Australian animals, offering plenty of chances for children to interact with the animals and learn about their care and protection.

6. Luna Park Sydney

While not a traditional museum or zoo, **Luna Park** is an interactive family destination in itself. Located in Milsons Point, this amusement park is filled with fun, hands-on activities for kids, including rides like roller coasters and carousels, as well as games and attractions that require interaction and skill. The park's **Giggle and Hoot Playland** is a great area for younger children, where they can enjoy fun rides and explore the interactive spaces designed just for them.

Location: 1 Olympic Dr, Milsons Point

Entry Price: Free entry, Ride tickets: $10–$20 per ride

Contact: +61 2 9922 1640

Why Visit: Luna Park's interactive nature and fun rides make it a fantastic place for families to enjoy a day of amusement and excitement.

7. Australian National Maritime Museum

The **Australian National Maritime Museum** offers interactive exhibits on Australia's maritime history, with hands-on activities for children. Kids can explore historical ships, learn how to sail in a virtual environment, and even experience a submarine. The museum often hosts workshops and interactive programs where kids can build their own boats or discover the stories of Australia's famous explorers.

Location: 2 Murray St, Darling Harbour

Entry Price: Adults $25, Children (4-16 years) $15, Children under 4 years: Free

Contact: +61 2 9298 3777

Why Visit: The museum is perfect for young explorers, offering interactive experiences like virtual sailing and ship tours that help children understand Australia's maritime history.

8. Australian Centre for Photography

The **Australian Centre for Photography** offers families a chance to engage in interactive photography workshops. The center features exhibitions and provides hands-on programs for children to learn photography skills. It offers a unique opportunity for kids to explore the world of art and photography through creative workshops and guided activities.
Location: 72-74 Oxford St, Paddington

Entry Price: Varies by exhibition, typically free for children

Contact: +61 2 9332 1455

Why Visit: This is a perfect spot for budding photographers, offering interactive experiences that inspire creativity in children.

Final Thoughts

Sydney offers a wealth of interactive museums and zoos that provide educational and fun experiences for the whole family. Whether it's exploring marine life at the SEA LIFE Aquarium, getting close to Australian wildlife at Taronga Zoo, or engaging in science experiments at the Powerhouse Museum, there's no shortage of places where kids can learn while playing.

These attractions not only entertain but also spark curiosity and help foster a deeper understanding of the world around them.

7.3   Kid-Friendly Beaches and Parks

Sydney is famous for its stunning beaches and beautiful parks, making it an ideal city for families to enjoy the outdoors. Whether your kids love to swim, play, or explore nature, Sydney's beaches and parks offer something for everyone. Here's a look at some of the best kid-friendly beaches and parks around the city:

---

1. Bondi Beach

Bondi Beach is one of Sydney's most iconic beaches and a great spot for families. The beach is safe for kids with its designated swimming areas that are patrolled by lifeguards. Children can also enjoy the rock pools, which are perfect for wading and discovering marine life. The Bondi to Coogee coastal walk offers stunning views, and there are plenty of cafes and playgrounds nearby for a family-friendly atmosphere.

Location: Bondi Beach, Eastern Suburbs

Why Visit: Safe swimming areas, rock pools for kids, cafes and playgrounds, family-friendly coastal walk.

2. Coogee Beach

Coogee Beach is another popular, family-friendly beach with calm waters perfect for kids. The beach is often less crowded than Bondi, offering a more relaxed atmosphere. The **Coogee Family Picnic Area** provides picnic tables, BBQ facilities, and a large grassy space for children to run around. There is also a shallow water area for safe swimming and paddling.

Location: Coogee, Eastern Suburbs

Why Visit: Calm waters, picnic areas, shallow swimming zones, and a relaxed, family-friendly environment.

3. Manly Beach

Manly Beach is a family favorite with a wide range of activities for kids. The **Manly Surf School** offers surf lessons for children, and the beach has a designated swimming area that is safe and patrolled by lifeguards. Manly's **Oceanworld Aquarium** and **Manly's Ocean Beachfront** provide additional fun for families. The nearby **Manly Scenic Walkway** is perfect for a family hike with stunning views.

Location: Manly, Northern Beaches

Why Visit: Surfing lessons for kids, safe swimming areas, family-friendly attractions like the aquarium.

4. Sydney Park

Sydney Park, located in St Peters, is one of the best parks for kids in the city. The park features wide open spaces, a fantastic playground with climbing structures, swings, and sandpits, as well as plenty of paths for cycling and walking. The **bike tracks** and **water play area** are great for active kids, and there are plenty of shaded areas for a picnic.

Location: St Peters, Inner West

Why Visit: Huge playgrounds, bike tracks, water play area, and open spaces perfect for family picnics.

5. Centennial Parklands

Centennial Park is one of Sydney's most popular green spaces, perfect for a family day out. Kids can explore the park on foot, by bike, or even on horseback. The **Centennial Park Nature Walk** and **explorer tours** are engaging for children, and the park's **playgrounds** offer plenty of fun equipment for all ages. There are also large ponds with ducks and swans, making it a peaceful and picturesque place to visit.

Location: Centennial Park, Eastern Suburbs

Why Visit: Horse riding, nature walks, large playgrounds, and picturesque picnic areas.

6. Royal Botanic Garden Sydney

The **Royal Botanic Garden** offers a peaceful, familyfriendly escape right next to the Sydney Opera House. The **Children's Garden** is a highlight, where kids can engage with nature through interactive play areas such as a waterplay area, climbing structures, and a maze. The garden also features open spaces for running, kite flying, and picnics, making it a great spot to unwind with the family.

Location: Mrs Macquaries Rd, Sydney

Why Visit: Children's garden, beautiful outdoor spaces, interactive play, and close proximity to major attractions like the Opera House.

7.4 Fun Activities for Kids: Sydney Tower Eye & Amusement Parks

Sydney offers a variety of fun activities that will thrill kids and keep them entertained. From towering views of the city to exciting amusement parks, here are some must-try activities for children in Sydney:

1. Sydney Tower Eye

The **Sydney Tower Eye** offers one of the best views of the city, and it's a thrilling experience for kids. At 309 meters tall, the Tower provides panoramic views of Sydney's skyline, the harbour, and surrounding areas. For an added adventure, the **Skywalk** experience allows kids to walk around the open-air observation deck while safely harnessed, giving them an exciting 360-degree view of the city. Kids can also enjoy interactive exhibits and educational displays in the building's interactive zone.

Location: 100 Market St, Sydney

Entry Price: Adults $30, Children (4-15 years) $20, Children under 4 years: Free

Contact: +61 2 9333 9222

Why Visit: Spectacular views of Sydney, fun interactive experiences, and the Skywalk for a thrilling adventure.

2. Luna Park Sydney

Luna Park in Milsons Point is Sydney's iconic amusement park. It offers a fun-filled day for families, with rides, games, and attractions for all ages. Kids can enjoy the **Carousel**, the **Ferris wheel**, and the **Big Dipper** roller coaster. There are also plenty of games to win prizes and family-friendly shows throughout the day. The park's lively atmosphere and beautiful location by the harbour make it a must-visit for families.

Location: 1 Olympic Dr, Milsons Point

Entry Price: Free entry, Rides from $10–$20 per ride

Contact: +61 2 9922 1640

Why Visit: Fun rides, games, and family-friendly entertainment with beautiful harbour views.

3. Taronga Zoo Sydney

Taronga Zoo is one of the best family-friendly attractions in Sydney, offering both education and excitement for kids. The zoo features a wide variety of animals from around the world, and children can participate in interactive exhibits, animal feedings, and educational programs. The **Wild Ropes Adventure** is an exciting experience that lets kids climb and navigate through the treetops, while the **Zoo Adventures** program offers hands-on learning about animal conservation and wildlife.

Location: Bradleys Head Rd, Mosman

Entry Price: Adults $49, Children (4-15 years) $29, Children under 4 years: Free

Contact: +61 2 9969 2777

Why Visit: Animal encounters, Wild Ropes Adventure, and hands-on learning programs make it a perfect spot for kids.

4. Sydney Olympic Park

Sydney Olympic Park offers a wide range of activities for children, from outdoor play areas to cycling tracks. The **Bubba's Garden** is a great spot for young children to explore nature, while the **Aquatic Centre** has water play areas and pools suitable for kids. For those looking for adventure, the **TreeTop Adventure Park** offers an exciting treetop challenge with rope courses and zip lines, perfect for active families.

Location: Sydney Olympic Park, Homebush Bay

Entry Price: Varies by activity (TreeTop Adventure starts at $25)

Contact: +61 2 9714 7888

Why Visit: Play areas, water parks, cycling tracks, and treetop adventure courses make it ideal for a fun family day out.

Final Thoughts

Sydney is a fantastic destination for families, with a wealth of kid-friendly beaches and parks to explore, as well as a variety of fun-filled activities. Whether it's enjoying the calm waters of Coogee Beach, exploring nature in Centennial Park, or experiencing the thrill of Luna Park, Sydney provides countless opportunities for kids to have fun and learn. These outdoor adventures and attractions wil

8. Shopping and Souvenirs

8.1 Best Shopping Streets and Districts in Sydney

Sydney is a shopper's paradise, offering a variety of options from luxury boutiques to unique, independent stores and vibrant markets. Whether you're after highend fashion, quirky gifts, or locally made products, Sydney's shopping streets and districts have something for everyone. Here are the best places to shop in Sydney:

---

1. Pitt Street Mall

Pitt Street Mall is one of Sydney's most famous shopping destinations, located in the heart of the city's Central Business District (CBD). This pedestrian-only street is lined with major department stores, high-end fashion brands, and popular retail chains. It's the place to go for fashion, electronics, beauty products, and more. Some of the flagship stores on Pitt Street Mall include **David Jones**, **Myer**, and **Apple Store**, as well as popular fashion retailers like **Uniqlo** and **Zara**. **Location**: Pitt Street, CBD

Why Visit: Major shopping hub with a wide range of stores, from luxury brands to high-street fashion.

---

2. Queen Victoria Building (QVB)

The **Queen Victoria Building** (QVB) is one of Sydney's most iconic shopping destinations, housed in a beautiful, heritage-listed building dating back to the 19th century. Inside, you'll find a selection of luxury boutiques, designer stores, and specialty shops. The QVB also features a variety of cafes and eateries, making it a great place for a break after shopping. It's the perfect destination if you're looking for a more upscale and elegant shopping experience.

Location: 455 George Street, CBD

Why Visit: Beautiful architecture, luxury shopping, and a selection of specialty stores.

---

3. Oxford Street

Oxford Street is the go-to shopping district for those looking for trendy fashion and independent boutiques. Stretching from Darlinghurst to Paddington, it's full of stylish stores, art galleries, cafes, and vintage shops. The area is known for its high-end fashion, but you'll also find local Australian designers and unique homeware stores. **Paddington Markets** (held on Saturdays) is another highlight, where you can shop for handmade goods, jewelry, clothing, and unique souvenirs.

Location: Oxford Street, Darlinghurst to Paddington

Why Visit: Trendy boutiques, local Australian designers, and vintage stores.

4. The Rocks

For a more historic shopping experience, head to **The Rocks**. This historic area is home to a mix of charming cobblestone streets, markets, and small, unique stores selling everything from local art to handmade jewelry and Australian souvenirs. The **Rocks Markets** (held on weekends) are a must-visit for unique, one-of-akind products like Aboriginal art, locally crafted leather goods, and designer accessories. The area also has cozy cafes, pubs, and a range of small galleries that showcase local artists.

Location: The Rocks, near Circular Quay

Why Visit: Historic charm, local art, handmade goods, and the weekend markets for unique souvenirs.

---

5. Bondi Junction

If you're staying near Bondi Beach, **Bondi Junction** is an excellent shopping destination. This shopping district features the **Westfield Bondi Junction**, a large shopping center that houses both international retailers and Australian brands. You'll find a mix of fashion stores, beauty shops, homeware outlets, and electronics. Bondi Junction is also home to plenty of dining options, making it perfect for a shopping trip combined with a meal or two.

Location: Bondi Junction, Eastern Suburbs

Why Visit: Large shopping mall with a variety of stores, including high-street fashion and homeware brands.

---

6. Glebe Markets

If you're looking for something a little different, the **Glebe Markets** are a must-visit. Held every Saturday, these lively markets offer a range of second-hand clothes, vintage fashion, handmade crafts, and unique souvenirs. It's the perfect place to find quirky, one-ofa-kind items and treasure hunts for bargains. The market also features delicious food stalls, so you can grab a bite while you shop.

Location: Glebe, Inner West

Why Visit: Vintage fashion, unique handmade goods, and second-hand treasures.

---

7. Surry Hills

Surry Hills is another hotspot for independent boutiques and unique fashion finds. Known for its creative and artistic vibe, the area is full of stylish shops selling everything from modern fashion to vintage clothing, accessories, and home decor. You'll also find a number of high-end furniture and design stores. Surry Hills is also known for its vibrant café culture, so after shopping, you can relax in one of the many trendy cafés in the area.

Location: Surry Hills, Eastern Suburbs

Why Visit: Independent boutiques, vintage stores, design shops, and a great café culture.

8. Marrickville Metro

For those interested in a more laid-back shopping experience, **Marrickville Metro** is a local favorite. Located in the inner-west of Sydney, this area has a mix of Asian supermarkets, trendy clothing stores, and unique international goods. Marrickville is also home to a thriving food scene, with local cafes and restaurants offering delicious meals to enjoy after a day of shopping.

Location: Marrickville, Inner West

Why Visit: Local shopping mall with a mix of international goods, unique stores, and food options.

9. Westfield Sydney

Located in the heart of the city, **Westfield Sydney** is a large shopping center with a great selection of highstreet fashion, luxury brands, and local Australian designers. It's a great spot to find clothing, shoes, accessories, and cosmetics. Westfield Sydney also boasts a variety of dining options, ranging from quick bites to fine dining, and is perfect for a full day of shopping and eating.

Location: Pitt Street Mall, Sydney CBD

Why Visit: Large selection of fashion brands, luxury stores, and dining options in the heart of the city.

10. Paddington Markets

Paddington Markets are a local favorite and a great place to shop for handmade and artisan products. These markets have been running since 1973 and feature local designers, artists, and craftspeople. You can shop for jewelry, homewares, clothing, and accessories, all made by local artisans. Paddington Markets is also a wonderful place to pick up unique souvenirs that you won't find anywhere else.

Location: Paddington, Eastern Suburbs

Why Visit: Handmade goods, artisan jewelry, and local designer clothing.

Final Thoughts

Sydney's shopping streets and districts are as diverse as the city itself. From high-end fashion and luxury shopping in **Pitt Street Mall** and **QVB** to unique markets and vintage finds in **The Rocks** and **Glebe Markets**, there's something for every type of shopper. Whether you're looking for designer brands, handmade products, or quirky local treasures, Sydney's shopping districts are sure to offer an unforgettable shopping experience!

8.2 Markets and Souvenir Shops in Sydney

Sydney is home to a variety of markets that offer everything from fresh produce to unique souvenirs and handmade goods. These markets are perfect for picking up a memento of your trip, as well as discovering local art, crafts, and food. Whether you're searching for something special to take home or simply enjoying the lively atmosphere, Sydney's markets have something for every traveler.

1. The Rocks Markets

The **Rocks Markets** are one of Sydney's most iconic markets, set in the historic **The Rocks** district. Open every weekend, the market is a great place to find locally made arts and crafts, jewelry, clothing, homewares, and souvenirs. You'll also find a range of Aboriginal art, handmade leather goods, and unique designer pieces. With live music and food stalls offering delicious local treats, The Rocks Markets is the perfect place to spend a few hours soaking in the vibrant atmosphere.

Location: George Street, The Rocks

Open: Every Saturday and Sunday, 10:00 AM to 5:00 PM

Why Visit: Local arts and crafts, Aboriginal art, handmade jewelry, and unique souvenirs.

Price Range: $5 – $100+ depending on the item.

---

2. Paddington Markets

The **Paddington Markets** have been a staple in Sydney for over 40 years. These markets offer a fantastic range of handmade goods, from clothing and accessories to jewelry and home décor. It's a great spot for shopping for fashion pieces from local designers, as well as picking up one-of-a-kind souvenirs. The market also has a range of food vendors selling delicious treats, making it a great place for a weekend outing.
Location: 395 Oxford Street, Paddington

Open: Saturdays, 10:00 AM to 4:00 PM

Why Visit: Local designers, handmade fashion, and unique artisan souvenirs.

Price Range: $10 – $150 for designer goods.

---

3. Glebe Markets

Held every Saturday, the **Glebe Markets** are a favorite among locals and tourists alike for their second-hand clothes, vintage fashion, and quirky, handmade goods. The market also features unique homeware, vinyl records, and locally crafted products. If you're looking for vintage clothes, unique knickknacks, or retro collectibles, this market is the place to go. Don't forget to explore the food stalls offering international dishes and local delicacies!

Location: Glebe Public School, Glebe Point Road

Open: Saturdays, 10:00 AM to 4:00 PM

Why Visit: Vintage clothing, second-hand treasures, handmade crafts, and food stalls.

Price Range: $5 – $50 for vintage items and local products.

---

4. Bondi Markets

The **Bondi Markets** are held every Sunday and offer a mix of fashion, art, and local food. The market is located near the iconic Bondi Beach, making it a great place to browse and shop after a relaxing day by the sea. You'll find local fashion designers, handcrafted jewelry, art prints, and eco-friendly products, all set against the vibrant atmosphere of Bondi. It's the perfect place for casual shopping and finding unique, locally made souvenirs.

Location: Bondi Beach Public School, Campbell Parade, Bondi

Open: Sundays, 10:00 AM to 4:00 PM

Why Visit: Eco-friendly products, local fashion, and handmade crafts.

Price Range: $10 – $75 for local fashion and accessories.

5. Eveleigh Market

If you're in the mood for fresh produce, locally grown products, and artisanal foods, the **Eveleigh Market** is a must-visit. This market, located in the trendy suburb of Redfern, specializes in organic produce, fresh flowers, gourmet foods, and eco-friendly products. While it's not necessarily a souvenir market, it's an excellent place to pick up food-related items like homemade jams, sauces, and fresh herbs as gifts to take home.

Location: Carriageworks, 245 Wilson Street, Eveleigh

Open: Saturdays, 8:00 AM to 1:00 PM

Why Visit: Organic produce, artisan foods, fresh flowers, and sustainable products.

Price Range: $5 – $40 for fresh produce and artisanal foods.

---

6. Sydney Fish Market

For those looking to take home a unique souvenir from Sydney's seafood capital, the **Sydney Fish Market** offers not only an incredible range of fresh seafood but also cooking supplies, specialty sauces, and even seafood-themed gifts. The market is a local icon and the largest seafood market in the Southern
Hemisphere, with a variety of shops selling fresh fish, oysters, and other marine delicacies. It's the perfect stop for seafood lovers looking to bring home the best of Sydney's aquatic offerings.

Location: 1 Bank Street, Pyrmont

Open: Every day, 5:00 AM to 4:00 PM

Why Visit: Fresh seafood, cooking supplies, seafoodrelated gifts, and local delicacies.

Price Range: $10 – $200 for seafood, sauces, and cooking items.

---

7. The Calypso Market

Located in the heart of **Kings Cross**, the **Calypso Market** offers a unique blend of arts, crafts, and vintage goods. This smaller market has a laid-back vibe, offering beautiful locally made jewelry, art prints, handcrafted goods, and antiques. It's perfect for those looking to find more niche and creative souvenirs to take home, including vintage furniture, retro items, and indie art.

Location: 102 Darlinghurst Road, Kings Cross

Open: Sundays, 10:00 AM to 4:00 PM

Why Visit: Indie art, vintage items, and unique handcrafted goods.

Price Range: $5 – $100 for antiques, vintage finds, and handmade crafts.

Final Thoughts

Sydney's markets offer an excellent way to experience the city's creative and local culture while shopping for souvenirs. From iconic markets like **The Rocks** and **Paddington Markets** to more niche spots like **Glebe Markets** and **Eveleigh Market**, there's no shortage of options for finding unique gifts and mementos. Whether you're looking for handmade goods, vintage fashion, or locally sourced food, Sydney's markets are an essential stop for any traveler.

8.3 Designer Boutiques and Luxury Shopping in Sydney

Sydney is home to some of the best luxury shopping destinations in the Southern Hemisphere. Whether you're seeking designer fashion, high-end jewelry, or premium homeware, Sydney's upscale boutiques and shopping districts offer an impressive range of luxury items. From international brands to local designers, Sydney's luxury shopping scene is perfect for those looking to indulge in world-class products.

---

1. Queen Victoria Building (QVB)

The **Queen Victoria Building (QVB)** is one of Sydney's most iconic shopping centers and a must-visit for luxury shoppers. Located in the heart of the city, the building itself is an architectural masterpiece, with its grand design and beautiful stained glass windows. Inside, you'll find an impressive range of high-end boutiques and designer stores, including **Louis Vuitton**, **Gucci**, **Chanel**, **Tiffany & Co.**, and **Prada**. Whether you're looking for luxury fashion, fine jewelry, or elegant accessories, the QVB is the ultimate destination for designer shopping.

Location: 455 George Street, Sydney

Why Visit: Luxury shopping in a historic setting, international designer brands.

Price Range: $100 – $10,000+ for designer clothing, accessories, and jewelry.

---

2. Pitt Street Mall

Pitt Street Mall is one of the busiest and most wellknown shopping districts in Sydney, offering a blend of high-end retailers and luxury boutiques. Along with international chains, you'll also find stores for **Armani**, **Burberry**, **Fendi**, and **Saint Laurent**, making it an ideal location for fashionistas seeking the latest trends. It's also home to **Myer** and **David Jones**, two of Australia's most famous department stores, which carry luxury brands, high-end fashion, and designer collections.

Location: Pitt Street, Sydney (between Market Street and King Street)

Why Visit: Top international luxury brands, vibrant shopping atmosphere.

Price Range: $150 – $5,000+ depending on the designer.

---

3. Westfield Sydney

Westfield Sydney, located on the corner of Pitt and Market Street, is another shopping haven offering luxury boutiques and designer fashion. Inside the multi-story complex, you'll find an impressive collection of high-end brands like **Balenciaga**, **Christian Louboutin**, **Dior**, and **Versace**. This mall provides an exceptional shopping experience with both local and international luxury offerings, making it a great place to find unique items or shop for the latest fashion trends.

Location: 188 Pitt Street, Sydney

Why Visit: Designer labels, exclusive collections, and modern shopping experience.

Price Range: $150 – $10,000+ for luxury fashion and accessories.

4. Paddington's Oxford Street

For those who love to explore chic boutiques, **Oxford Street** in **Paddington** is a great place for designer shopping with a touch of uniqueness. Here you'll find both established international labels and local Australian designers. Stores like **Zimmermann**, **Alice McCall**, and **Camilla and Marc** offer luxurious, high-quality pieces that reflect the vibrant style of Sydney's fashion scene. Paddington also offers an excellent selection of independent stores that feature curated collections of high-end products, from clothes to homewares.

Location: Oxford Street, Paddington

Why Visit: Trendy boutiques, Australian designers, and unique finds.

Price Range: $200 – $2,500+ for luxury fashion and accessories.

---

5. The Strand Arcade

The **Strand Arcade** is a historic shopping arcade in the heart of Sydney, offering an elegant and timeless shopping experience. Home to several Australian luxury brands, as well as international names, it's the perfect place for those looking for something exclusive. The arcade houses stores such as **Tiffany & Co.**, **Mimco**, and **Aesop**, offering fine jewelry, leather goods, and luxury skincare products. The charming Victorian-style architecture and refined ambiance make it an enjoyable destination for discerning shoppers.

Location: 412-414 George Street, Sydney

Why Visit: Historic shopping experience, Australian luxury brands, elegant ambiance.

Price Range: $50 – $5,000+ for jewelry, accessories, and designer goods.

8.4 Unique Souvenirs to Take Home from Sydney

When you visit Sydney, you'll want to take home something that reminds you of the city's unique culture, stunning landscapes, and creative spirit. From locally made arts and crafts to iconic Australian items, Sydney offers a wide variety of memorable souvenirs that reflect the essence of this vibrant city. Here are some of the best souvenirs to bring home from your Sydney trip.

---

1. Aboriginal Art and Artifacts

Sydney is rich in Aboriginal culture, and purchasing **Aboriginal art** or **artifacts** is a meaningful way to take home a piece of the country's history. You can find original artworks and crafts at galleries, markets, and cultural centers. Look for traditional dot paintings, handcrafted boomerangs, didgeridoos, and woven baskets. **The Art Gallery of New South Wales** and **The Rocks Markets** are excellent places to find authentic Aboriginal art pieces.

Price Range: $20 – $5,000+ depending on the size and rarity of the artwork.

---

2. Australian Wool and Merino Wool Products

Australia is famous for its **Merino wool**, and Sydney offers a variety of shops selling high-quality wool products such as scarves, sweaters, and blankets. You can find these items in luxury stores, boutique shops, and markets like **Paddington Markets**. Merino wool is soft, durable, and perfect for colder climates, making it an excellent souvenir to bring home.

Price Range: $50 – $300+ for wool scarves, sweaters, and blankets.

3. Australian Native Beauty Products

Sydney is home to a variety of beauty brands that use native Australian ingredients, such as **Tea Tree Oil**, **Kakadu Plum**, and **Macadamia Oil**. These ingredients are known for their natural healing properties and are often found in skincare products. Stores like **Aesop**, **Lush**, and **Jurlique** offer luxury beauty products that make for a lovely souvenir. You can also find natural skincare and body care products at **The Rocks Markets**.

Price Range: $15 – $150+ for skincare, haircare, and beauty products.

4. Opals and Australian Jewelry

Australia is renowned for its **opals**, and you can find beautiful opal jewelry in Sydney's jewelry stores and markets. Whether you're looking for earrings, rings, or necklaces, opals make for a stunning and unique souvenir that captures the beauty of the Australian outback. The **Queen Victoria Building** and **The Strand Arcade** feature several high-end jewelry stores offering opal pieces.

Price Range: $100 – $10,000+ for opal jewelry, depending on the size and quality of the stones.

5. Sydney-Themed Memorabilia

For those looking for classic tourist souvenirs, **Sydney-themed memorabilia** such as **Miniature Opera House models**, **Harbour Bridge keychains**, and **Sydney postcards** are easy to find. These small and affordable items make great keepsakes to remember your time in Sydney.

Price Range: $5 – $30 for keychains, souvenirs, and memorabilia.

Final Thoughts

Sydney offers a variety of luxury shopping options, from designer boutiques and department stores to local artisan markets, ensuring that every traveler can find something special to take home. Whether you're splurging on high-end fashion, picking up unique Australian crafts, or discovering rare opals, Sydney's shopping scene is sure to delight.

9. Accommodation in Sydney

9.1 Luxury Hotels and Resorts in Sydney

Sydney is home to a number of world-class luxury hotels and resorts, offering unparalleled service, stunning views, and prime locations. Whether you're seeking a waterfront retreat with views of the Sydney Opera House or a chic urban hotel in the heart of the city, Sydney has something for every taste and budget.

Here are some of the best luxury hotels and resorts to consider for your stay.

---

1. The Langham, Sydney

Located in the historic Rocks district, **The Langham, Sydney** offers a five-star experience with exceptional service and elegant interiors. The hotel is renowned for its luxurious accommodations, spa, and fine dining. Its central location means you're within walking distance of Sydney's top attractions, including Circular Quay and the Sydney Opera House. The rooms are designed to offer ultimate comfort, with spacious layouts and premium amenities.

Location: 89-113 Kent Street, The Rocks, Sydney

Why Stay: Exceptional luxury, historic building, world-class spa, and fine dining.

Price Range: $400 – $1,500 per night

Contact: +61 2 9241 1833

---

2. Park Hyatt Sydney

The **Park Hyatt Sydney** is one of the most iconic luxury hotels in Sydney, offering stunning views of the Sydney Opera House and Harbour Bridge. This modern hotel features sleek and sophisticated interiors, large suites, and top-tier amenities. Guests can enjoy exclusive access to the hotel's rooftop pool, spa, and fine dining restaurant. Whether you're relaxing in your room or dining in style, the views and service here are second to none.

Location: 7 Hickson Road, The Rocks, Sydney

Why Stay: Stunning Opera House views, luxury service, exclusive location.

Price Range: $800 – $2,500 per night

Contact: +61 2 9256 1234

---

3. Four Seasons Hotel Sydney

With its prime location near Circular Quay and The Rocks, **Four Seasons Hotel Sydney** offers a blend of classic elegance and modern luxury. The hotel boasts spacious rooms, an outdoor pool with city views, a renowned spa, and several dining options, including the acclaimed **Mode Kitchen & Bar**. It's a great option for travelers seeking comfort and style, with a perfect location to explore the city's best attractions.

Location: 199 George Street, Sydney

Why Stay: Central location, luxurious facilities, topnotch dining options.

Price Range: $500 – $1,500 per night

Contact: +61 2 9250 3100

4. The Darling at The Star

Located in Pyrmont, **The Darling** at The Star is a fivestar hotel that exudes elegance and contemporary design. It is part of the larger **The Star Sydney** complex, which includes a casino, world-class restaurants, and bars. The hotel offers luxurious rooms with floor-to-ceiling windows, a spa, and a rooftop pool with panoramic views. This hotel is perfect for those looking for a chic, modern stay with entertainment at their doorstep.

Location: 80 Pyrmont Street, Pyrmont, Sydney

Why Stay: Modern luxury, casino and entertainment complex, stunning views.

Price Range: $400 – $1,200 per night

Contact: +61 2 9657 8000

5. InterContinental Sydney

The **InterContinental Sydney** is a grand and historic hotel set within a former Treasury Building. Situated overlooking Sydney Harbour, the hotel combines heritage charm with modern comforts. The rooms are spacious, and the hotel features an outdoor pool, multiple dining options, and an iconic rooftop bar with stunning views. It's the perfect choice for those who want a refined luxury experience in a central location.

Location: 117 Macquarie Street, Sydney

Why Stay: Historic building, prime location, luxury service, stunning views.

Price Range: $450 – $1,500 per night

Contact: +61 2 9240 8888

---

6. Crown Towers Sydney

Located within **Crown Sydney**, the newest and most luxurious resort in Barangaroo, **Crown Towers Sydney** offers an extraordinary experience for its guests. The hotel features ultra-modern design, spacious rooms, and luxury facilities such as an infinity pool overlooking the harbor, a high-end spa, and a selection of gourmet dining options. The views of the city skyline and the Harbour Bridge are spectacular, making it a top choice for those seeking unparalleled luxury.

Location: 1 Barangaroo Avenue, Barangaroo, Sydney

Why Stay: Ultra-modern luxury, exceptional service, stunning views.

Price Range: $900 – $2,500 per night

Contact: +61 2 8870 1000

---

7. The Woollahra Hotel

Nestled in the leafy eastern suburbs of Sydney, **The Woollahra Hotel** offers a more intimate, boutiquestyle luxury experience. Known for its sophisticated design, cozy rooms, and impeccable service, this hotel is ideal for travelers who want a peaceful, stylish stay away from the hustle and bustle of the city center. The hotel's in-house bar and restaurant offer a wonderful local dining experience as well.

Location: 117 Queen Street, Woollahra, Sydney

Why Stay: Boutique luxury, peaceful location, chic interiors.

Price Range: $350 – $1,000 per night

Contact: +61 2 9327 1166

Conclusion

Sydney's luxury hotels and resorts cater to a wide range of tastes, offering everything from historic charm to modern design and stunning views. Whether you're looking for a grand hotel with all the amenities or a more intimate boutique experience, Sydney has something to offer. With their world-class service, prime locations, and luxurious amenities, these hotels ensure that your stay in Sydney will be unforgettable.

9.2 Budget-Friendly Accommodation Options in Sydney

Sydney, being a popular travel destination, offers a wide range of accommodations for different budgets. While the city is known for its luxury resorts and hotels, there are plenty of budget-friendly options that still provide comfort, great service, and prime locations. Whether you're a solo traveler, a couple, or a family, here are some great budget options to consider during your stay in Sydney.

1. The Capsule Hotel

Located in the heart of the city, **The Capsule Hotel** offers an affordable and unique stay with modern, compact rooms designed in a minimalist Japanese capsule style. It's ideal for solo travelers looking for a clean, private space at a fraction of the price of traditional hotels. The hotel also features a communal kitchen and lounge area for guests to socialize. It's located within walking distance of Sydney Central Station, making it a convenient base for exploring the city.

Location: 5/44-46 Elizabeth Street, Sydney

Why Stay: Affordable, unique capsule-style rooms, central location.

Price Range: $60 – $120 per night

Contact: +61 2 9267 1377

---

2. Ibis Budget Sydney East

Ibis Budget Sydney East is a no-frills, budget-friendly hotel located in the Darlinghurst area. It offers simple rooms with all the basic amenities needed for a comfortable stay, including free Wi-Fi, air conditioning, and a 24-hour front desk. The hotel is conveniently located near public transportation and is just a short distance from popular attractions like Bondi Beach, the Royal Botanic Gardens, and the Opera House.

Location: 5-7 Elizabet Bay Road, Darlinghurst, Sydney

Why Stay: Budget-friendly, great location, free Wi-Fi.

Price Range: $80 – $140 per night

Contact: +61 2 9361 4577

---

3. Sydney Harbour YHA

For travelers looking for an affordable, social atmosphere, **Sydney Harbour YHA** is a great option. This modern hostel is located in the historic Rocks area, offering easy access to iconic sites like the Sydney Opera House and Circular Quay. The hostel provides dormitory-style accommodations as well as private rooms, with shared kitchen and bathroom facilities. The rooftop terrace offers spectacular views of Sydney Harbour and the Opera House.

Location: 110 Cumberland Street, The Rocks, Sydney

Why Stay: Affordable, social atmosphere, stunning views of Sydney Harbour.

Price Range: $40 – $100 per night (for dorms) / $120 – $200 per night (for private rooms)

Contact: +61 2 9247 5084

---

4. The Merrymaker Hostel

Located in the vibrant area of Surry Hills, **The Merrymaker Hostel** offers budget-friendly accommodation with a lively atmosphere. The hostel is a great option for young travelers and backpackers. It offers dormitory rooms and private rooms with shared bathrooms, as well as a communal kitchen and lounge areas where guests can relax and meet fellow travelers. The area is known for its cafes, restaurants, and nightlife.

Location: 4/82-84 Cleveland Street, Surry Hills, Sydney

Why Stay: Social atmosphere, affordable, close to cafes and nightlife.

Price Range: $50 – $100 per night (for dorms) / $120 – $180 per night (for private rooms)

Contact: +61 2 9699 3434

5. Wake Up! Sydney Central

Wake Up! Sydney Central is a modern, affordable backpacker hostel that's ideal for young travelers looking for a fun, social stay. Located near Central Station, the hostel is well-connected to all of Sydney's major attractions. It offers dormitory-style rooms and private rooms, as well as a range of amenities including free Wi-Fi, a bar, a cafe, and a travel desk to help guests plan their activities. The vibrant atmosphere makes it easy to meet other travelers.

Location: 509 Pitt Street, Sydney

Why Stay: Great for backpackers, vibrant social atmosphere, close to public transport.

Price Range: $40 – $100 per night (for dorms) / $120 – $220 per night (for private rooms)

Contact: +61 2 9211 8744

6. Hotel ibis Sydney World Square

The **Ibis Sydney World Square** offers excellent value for money and is a great choice for budget travelers who want a comfortable, central place to stay. Located in the city center, it's close to shopping areas, dining options, and major transport hubs. The rooms are compact but well-appointed with modern amenities, and the hotel features a 24-hour front desk and a restaurant. It's perfect for those who want to stay close to the action without breaking the bank.

Location: 382-384 Pitt Street, Haymarket, Sydney

Why Stay: Budget-friendly, central location, great for business or leisure.

Price Range: $100 – $180 per night

Contact: +61 2 9214 0700

7. Manly Backpackers

For a more laid-back, beachside stay, **Manly Backpackers** is a great budget option. Located near Manly Beach, it's ideal for travelers who want to enjoy Sydney's beaches without staying in the city center. The hostel offers dormitory rooms and private rooms with shared bathrooms, as well as a communal kitchen and lounge area. The location is perfect for those who want to surf, swim, or explore the stunning coastal walks around Manly.

Location: 39 The Corso, Manly, Sydney

Why Stay: Close to the beach, affordable, great for surf lovers.

Price Range: $50 – $120 per night (for dorms) / $120 – $200 per night (for private rooms)

Contact: +61 2 9977 0977

Conclusion

Sydney offers many budget-friendly accommodation options that provide good value without sacrificing comfort. From hostels and backpacker havens to budget hotels in the city center and beachside areas, there's something for everyone. Whether you prefer to stay in a lively social environment or need a quiet retreat, Sydney has affordable options to fit your needs and ensure a comfortable and enjoyable stay.

9.3 Family and GroupFriendly Hotels in Sydney

Sydney is a fantastic destination for families and groups, with plenty of hotels offering spacious accommodations and family-friendly amenities. These hotels cater to the needs of families and groups, ensuring everyone has a comfortable and enjoyable stay. Here are some great options for family and groupfriendly hotels in Sydney:

---

1. Novotel Sydney on Darling Harbour

The **Novotel Sydney on Darling Harbour** is a popular family-friendly hotel offering spacious rooms and excellent facilities. Located just a short walk from major attractions like the SEA LIFE Sydney Aquarium, the Australian National Maritime Museum, and the Powerhouse Museum, this hotel is ideal for families exploring the city. The hotel features family rooms with plenty of space, an outdoor pool, a kids' club, and a range of dining options, making it a great choice for families.

Location: 100 Murray Street, Pyrmont, Sydney

Why Stay: Great location near family attractions, outdoor pool, kids' club, family rooms.

Price Range: $250 – $450 per night (family rooms)

Contact: +61 2 9288 7188

---

2. The Langham, Sydney

The Langham, Sydney offers luxury accommodations with a family-friendly touch. Located in The Rocks, it's close to many of Sydney's iconic attractions like Circular Quay and the Sydney Opera House. The hotel features spacious suites, some of which are perfect for families or small groups, as well as kid-friendly amenities like babysitting services, a kids' pool, and a family concierge to assist with planning activities. The Langham also offers family packages with added perks like tickets to local attractions.

Location: 89-113 Kent Street, The Rocks, Sydney

Why Stay: Luxurious, spacious suites, family concierge, close to attractions.

Price Range: $500 – $700 per night (suites)

Contact: +61 2 8256 2222

3. Rydges Sydney Central

Rydges Sydney Central offers a family-friendly stay with spacious rooms and a central location. It's within walking distance to Central Station, making it easy to access major attractions and public transport. Families can enjoy the hotel's large rooms, an outdoor swimming pool, and the option of family suites. There are also dining options and a relaxed atmosphere, perfect for families with young children.

Location: 28 Albion Street, Surry Hills, Sydney

Why Stay: Spacious family suites, close to Central Station, pool, relaxed atmosphere.

Price Range: $200 – $350 per night (family suites)

Contact: +61 2 9318 3222

---

4. Holiday Inn Darling Harbour

The **Holiday Inn Darling Harbour** offers comfortable accommodations with convenient access to many family-friendly attractions in Sydney. It is just a short walk to places like Darling Harbour and the Chinese Garden of Friendship. The hotel provides family rooms with amenities like kids' meals, cribs, and an indoor pool. Families can also take advantage of the hotel's easy access to public transportation to explore the city.

Location: 68 Harbour Street, Haymarket, Sydney
Why Stay: Family rooms, close to Darling Harbour, indoor pool, kids' amenities.

Price Range: $180 – $350 per night (family rooms)

Contact: +61 2 9288 9988

---

5. Oaks Sydney Goldsbrough Suites

For larger groups or families needing extra space, **Oaks Sydney Goldsbrough Suites** offers fullyequipped apartments with kitchen facilities, living areas, and private bathrooms. The property features spacious one- and two-bedroom apartments, making it ideal for longer stays or those traveling with children. The hotel is located near Darling Harbour and the city's major shopping districts, and it offers a range of amenities including an indoor pool, gym, and concierge services.

Location: 243 Pyrmont Street, Pyrmont, Sydney

Why Stay: Spacious apartments, family-friendly amenities, close to Darling Harbour.

Price Range: $230 – $500 per night (apartments)

Contact: +61 2 9518 2400

9.4 Eco-Friendly and Sustainable Hotels in Sydney

Sydney is becoming increasingly focused on sustainability, and many hotels in the city are incorporating eco-friendly practices to help minimize their environmental impact. From green-certified accommodations to hotels with sustainable amenities, here are some great eco-friendly hotels in Sydney:

---

1. The Old Clare Hotel

The **Old Clare Hotel** is a stylish and eco-friendly hotel located in the heart of Chippendale. The hotel is built in a renovated historic building, combining oldworld charm with modern sustainability. The property has received recognition for its sustainable practices, including energy-efficient lighting, water-saving measures, and a strong commitment to reducing waste. It also has a green roof, which helps improve insulation and reduce energy consumption.

Location: 1 Kensington Street, Chippendale, Sydney

Why Stay: Sustainable design, eco-friendly practices, unique, stylish setting.

Price Range: $200 – $350 per night

Contact: +61 2 8277 1300

---

2. Ovolo Woolloomooloo

Ovolo Woolloomooloo is an eco-conscious luxury hotel offering a range of sustainable initiatives. The hotel has been designed with energy efficiency in mind, and it uses locally sourced, organic materials wherever possible. It also has an in-house sustainable dining experience, offers free bike rentals, and supports ecofriendly transportation options. The hotel's commitment to sustainability is reflected in its zerowaste approach, and it also participates in various local environmental programs.

Location: 6 Cowper Wharf Road, Woolloomooloo, Sydney

Why Stay: Sustainable design, eco-friendly amenities, great location near the harbour.

Price Range: $350 – $600 per night

Contact: +61 2 9331 9000

---

3. QT Sydney

QT Sydney blends modern luxury with eco-friendly practices. The hotel incorporates sustainable design features, including energy-efficient lighting and watersaving devices. It's also known for using locallysourced products and materials in its design and operations. Guests can enjoy the hotel's environmentally-conscious dining options, as well as participate in initiatives that promote sustainability throughout their stay.

Location: 49 Market Street, Sydney

Why Stay: Eco-conscious design, sustainable dining, luxury experience.

Price Range: $250 – $450 per night

Contact: +61 2 8262 0000

---

4. The Medusa Hotel

The Medusa Hotel offers a blend of boutique accommodation with a commitment to sustainability. This hotel is known for its green initiatives, including using energy-efficient appliances, eco-friendly cleaning products, and water-saving technologies. The hotel also offers bike rentals for guests who want to explore the city sustainably. The Medusa Hotel's focus on sustainability doesn't come at the cost of comfort, as it offers stylish rooms and personalized service.

Location: 267 Liverpool Street, Darlinghurst, Sydney

Why Stay: Green initiatives, eco-friendly rooms, central location.

Price Range: $150 – $250 per night

Contact: +61 2 9360 3211

---

5. Mercure Sydney

Mercure Sydney is committed to reducing its environmental impact by implementing various sustainability practices. The hotel features energyefficient heating and cooling systems, water-saving measures, and recycling programs. It also supports local farmers and sustainable agriculture through its in-house dining options. For guests looking to stay in a hotel with strong environmental practices while still enjoying comfort and convenience, Mercure Sydney is a great choice.

Location: 818-820 George Street, Haymarket, Sydney

Why Stay: Energy-efficient systems, local food sourcing, sustainability programs.

Price Range: $160 – $300 per night

Contact: +61 2 9217 6666

Conclusion

Sydney offers a wide range of family and group-friendly hotels, as well as eco-friendly options for those looking to reduce their environmental footprint. From luxury hotels with sustainable design to affordable family rooms, Sydney's accommodation options cater to all types of travelers. Whether you're traveling with kids, in a group, or seeking a more sustainable stay, these hotels provide comfort, convenience, and eco-conscious practices for a memorable stay in Australia's most iconic city.

10. Practical Information

<u>10.1 Essential Packing List for Sydney</u>

When preparing for your trip to Sydney, it's important to pack wisely to ensure you're ready for the city's diverse weather and outdoor activities. Here's a comprehensive packing list to help you make the most of your Sydney adventure in 2024-2025:

1. Weather-Appropriate Clothing

Sydney's climate is typically mild and sunny, but it can vary depending on the season, so it's essential to pack a range of clothes.

Summer (December to February): Light clothing like t-shirts, shorts, dresses, and swimwear. Don't forget sunglasses, a wide-brimmed hat, and sunscreen to protect yourself from the strong sun.

Autumn (March to May): Pack layers for the cooler evenings, such as light sweaters, jackets, and long pants. You may still want to bring swimwear if you plan on visiting the beach.

Winter (June to August): Sydney's winters are mild, but a light jacket or sweater is necessary. You may want to pack a raincoat as this is the wettest time of year.

Spring (September to November): Similar to autumn, layers are key. Pack a mix of warmer and lighter clothing, as temperatures can be quite changeable.

2. Swimwear

Sydney is famous for its stunning beaches, so don't forget to bring swimwear for a dip in Bondi, Manly, or any of the other beautiful beaches. Pack a towel if your accommodation doesn't provide one.

---

3. Comfortable Footwear

Sydney is a city best explored on foot, so comfortable shoes are essential. You'll likely be walking a lot, so pack a few different pairs for various activities:

Walking shoes: Comfortable sneakers or sandals for city sightseeing, walking tours, or hikes.

Flip-flops or water shoes: Perfect for the beach and other water activities.

Dress shoes: If you plan to dine at fine restaurants or attend a special event, bring a pair of dress shoes.

---

4. Outdoor and Adventure Gear

If you're planning on enjoying Sydney's many outdoor activities, you'll need to bring a few key items:

Hiking gear: If you're heading to the Blue Mountains or other hiking spots, make sure to pack sturdy hiking boots, a backpack, and a water bottle.

Sunscreen: The Australian sun can be harsh, so be sure to bring high-SPF sunscreen to protect your skin.

Hat and sunglasses: A wide-brimmed hat and UVprotective sunglasses will keep you safe from the sun.

Camera or phone: Sydney's scenic views and iconic landmarks like the Opera House and Harbour Bridge are perfect for photos.

5. Essentials for the Beach

If you plan to spend time at one of Sydney's famous beaches, packing a beach bag with these essentials is a must:

Towel: A beach towel for lounging by the water.

Swimwear: A swimsuit for swimming and relaxing by the beach.

Sunscreen: A waterproof sunscreen with a high SPF to protect against the sun's rays.

Water shoes: Optional, but helpful for rocky areas or surf conditions.

Flip-flops: For easy beachside footwear.

6. Electronics and Travel Gear

To make your trip easier, consider packing these essential electronics:

Portable charger: Ensure your phone and camera stay charged during sightseeing.

Travel adapter: Australia uses the Type I power plug, so bring an adapter if your devices are a different type.

Headphones: For flights, public transport, or relaxing in parks or cafes.

Camera/Smartphone: Capture all the beautiful moments in Sydney.

7. Personal Items

Don't forget the personal items that will make your trip comfortable and safe:

Medication: Bring any prescription medication you may need, along with a copy of the prescription in case you need to purchase more.

Toiletries: While hotels often provide basic toiletries, bring your preferred brands, especially if you're staying in more remote areas.

Reusable water bottle: Sydney has great tap water, so a reusable bottle will help you stay hydrated as you explore.

Hand sanitizer and wipes: For hygiene, especially when traveling around the city.

8. Health and Safety Items

Stay safe and healthy during your trip with these important items:

Face masks: Depending on the global situation or any health precautions, face masks may still be a good idea in crowded areas or on public transport.

First aid kit: A small first aid kit with band-aids, pain relief medication, antiseptic wipes, and any other basic items you may need.

Travel insurance: Ensure you have travel insurance that covers health issues, cancellations, and any potential issues during your stay.

---

9. Miscellaneous Items

Travel guidebook or map: While most people rely on their phones, it's helpful to have a physical guidebook or map for quick references or when in areas with limited reception.

Notebook and pen: For journaling or writing down useful information you pick up during your trip.

Backpack or day bag: For carrying your essentials when you go sightseeing, including snacks, water, sunscreen, and your camera.

---

10. Important Travel Documents

Passport: Ensure your passport is valid for at least 6 months from your planned departure date.

Visa: Australians require most international travelers to have a visa to visit. Make sure to check the visa requirements for your country.

Flight and accommodation details: Keep a copy of your booking confirmations, including addresses, check-in times, and emergency contact information.

Travel insurance: Always travel with insurance that covers medical emergencies, trip cancellation, and lost luggage.

Conclusion

Packing for Sydney requires a mix of clothes for various seasons, comfortable footwear for walking and outdoor activities, and the necessary personal items to stay healthy and safe. With these essentials, you'll be prepared for an unforgettable adventure in one of Australia's most exciting cities. Don't forget to pack a sense of adventure, as Sydney offers so much to explore!

10.2 Health and Safety Tips for Sydney

When traveling to Sydney, it's important to stay safe and healthy while you enjoy all the activities and sights. Below are some essential health and safety tips to help you have a safe and smooth trip.

---

1. Stay Hydrated

Sydney's warm climate, especially in summer, can lead to dehydration if you're not careful. Whether you're sightseeing, hiking, or spending time on the beach, it's important to drink plenty of water.

Tip: Carry a reusable water bottle with you, as tap water in Sydney is clean and safe to drink. You can refill your bottle at any public water fountain or your accommodation.

Average Cost: Water bottles at convenience stores or vending machines typically cost around AUD 2 to 3.

---

2. Protect Yourself from the Sun

The Australian sun can be intense, even on overcast days. To avoid sunburn and skin damage, make sure you take precautions:

Use Sunscreen: Apply sunscreen with a high SPF (30 or above) every few hours, especially when outdoors.

Wear a Hat and Sunglasses: A wide-brimmed hat and UV-protective sunglasses will protect your face and eyes.

Seek Shade: When the sun is at its strongest, typically between 10 AM and 4 PM, try to stay in the shade.

3. Know the Risks of the Ocean and Beaches

Sydney's beaches are beautiful but can also be dangerous, especially for swimmers who are unfamiliar with the conditions. Always pay attention to the safety warnings and follow the lifeguards' instructions.

Swim between the Flags: Lifeguarded beaches have red and yellow flags marking safe swimming zones. Never swim outside of these marked areas.

Rip Currents: Rip currents can be strong. If you're caught in one, don't panic—swim parallel to the shore to escape, then swim back to land.

Jellyfish: During the warmer months, jellyfish are common in some parts of Sydney. Be cautious, especially in the warmer months (October to May).

Many beaches provide stinger nets to protect swimmers.

---

4. Stay Safe in the City

Sydney is generally a safe city for tourists, but it's still important to stay aware of your surroundings:

Keep Your Belongings Safe: Always keep an eye on your bags and valuables, especially in busy areas like Circular Quay or Darling Harbour. Pickpocketing is rare, but it can still happen in crowded spots.

Avoid Isolated Areas at Night: Stick to well-lit, populated areas at night, and avoid walking alone in less-traveled places.

Emergency Contacts: In case of an emergency, dial 000 for police, fire, or medical emergencies.

---

5. Health Care and Insurance

While Sydney has excellent healthcare facilities, it's wise to have travel insurance that covers medical treatment in case of illness or injury. Here are some important health tips:

Travel Insurance: Make sure your travel insurance covers medical expenses and emergency medical evacuation.

Pharmacies: Sydney has plenty of pharmacies where you can buy over-the-counter medication for common issues like colds, headaches, or digestive problems. Some popular pharmacy chains include Chemist Warehouse and Priceline.

Medical Care: If you need a doctor, visit one of Sydney's walk-in clinics or private medical centers. For emergencies, head to a hospital's emergency department.

> **Sydney Hospitals**: Some of the well-known hospitals include St Vincent's Hospital (Darlinghurst) and Royal Prince Alfred Hospital (Camperdown).

6. Insect and Animal Safety

While Sydney is a wonderful place to explore nature, some insects and animals can pose risks, especially in outdoor and bushland areas:

Mosquitoes: Mosquitoes are common, especially in warmer months. Wear insect repellent, especially in areas with standing water or near parks and beaches.

Ticks: If you're hiking or exploring bushland areas, be aware of ticks. These can sometimes carry Lyme disease or cause allergic reactions.

Snakes and Spiders: Sydney is home to some potentially dangerous wildlife, including snakes and spiders. However, encounters are rare. If you're venturing into bushland or parks, wear closed shoes and be cautious.

7. Food and Water Safety

Sydney's food is generally very safe to eat, but like any big city, it's important to know some basic food and water safety tips:

Eat at Reputable Restaurants: Sydney has strict food safety regulations. To avoid food poisoning, choose restaurants with good reviews and reputable establishments.

Tap Water: Sydney's tap water is clean and safe to drink. In fact, it's some of the best tap water in the world! Always refill your water bottle from a tap rather than buying bottled water when possible.

8. Jet Lag and Time Zone Adjustment

Sydney is in the Australian Eastern Standard Time (AEST) zone, which can be quite different from your home time zone. Adjusting to the time difference can lead to jet lag, especially if you're coming from far away.

Tip: Try to adjust to the new time zone a few days before your trip. Avoid naps during the day, and get plenty of natural sunlight to help reset your internal clock.

Stay Active: Once you arrive in Sydney, try to stay active and hydrate, as this will help your body adjust quicker.

9. Respecting Local Laws and Customs

Sydney is an incredibly diverse city, and it's essential to respect the local culture and laws:

Smoking Laws: Smoking is banned in many public areas such as restaurants, beaches, and parks. Look for designated smoking areas.

Respect Aboriginal Culture: Sydney is built on land that holds deep cultural significance to the Aboriginal people. Be respectful of local traditions and heritage.

10. COVID-19 Guidelines and Health Protocols

Be sure to check the latest COVID-19 guidelines before traveling, as these can change based on the global situation. At the time of writing, Sydney has been following safety protocols to ensure the health of locals and tourists.

Masks: While masks are no longer mandatory in most public spaces, some venues may still require them, particularly in crowded indoor areas or public transport.

Health and Hygiene: Hand sanitizers are widely available, and cleaning protocols have been enhanced in public places.

Conclusion

By following these health and safety tips, you'll ensure that your time in Sydney is both enjoyable and safe. Staying hydrated, protecting yourself from the sun, and being mindful of your surroundings will help you make the most of your trip while keeping your health and well-being intact. Always remember to respect local customs and seek medical attention if necessary, and you'll have a great time exploring everything Sydney has to offer.

10.3 Emergency Contacts and Healthcare Services in

Sydney

When traveling, knowing where to turn in an emergency can make all the difference. Sydney, as a major international city, has a comprehensive system of emergency services and healthcare providers to ensure that help is always available when needed. Below are key emergency contacts and healthcare services you should be aware of during your trip.

1. Emergency Numbers

In case of any emergency—whether it's a medical situation, fire, or need for police assistance—you can reach the following emergency services:

Emergency Services (Police, Fire, Ambulance):
Phone Number: 000
This is the primary number to call for any emergency in Australia. Operators will direct your call to the appropriate service, such as the police, fire brigade, or ambulance. This number is free to dial from any phone, including mobile phones.

Non-Emergency Police Number:
Phone Number: 131 444
This number is for non-urgent police matters, like reporting lost items, minor incidents, or inquiries.

Mental Health Crisis Line:

Phone Number: 13 11 14
This 24/7 helpline offers support for individuals experiencing a mental health crisis, providing confidential assistance and information about mental health services.

---

2. Hospitals and Medical Centers in Sydney

Sydney has several well-equipped hospitals and medical centers for both emergencies and routine healthcare. Below are some of the major healthcare facilities in the city:

St Vincent's Hospital (Darlinghurst)
Address: 390 Victoria Street, Darlinghurst, NSW 2010
Phone Number: +61 2 8382 1111
A leading teaching hospital providing high-quality medical care, St Vincent's also has an emergency department for urgent medical cases.

Royal Prince Alfred Hospital (Camperdown)
Address: Missenden Road, Camperdown, NSW 2050
Phone Number: +61 2 9515 6111
RPA is one of Sydney's largest hospitals and is renowned for its emergency and trauma services. It also provides specialist services like cardiology, oncology, and more.

Sydney Children's Hospital (Randwick)
Address: High Street, Randwick, NSW 2031
Phone Number: +61 2 9382 1111

This hospital is dedicated to providing healthcare for children and adolescents. It includes a specialized emergency department for pediatric cases.

St George Hospital (Kogarah)
Address: 1-43 Kogarah Bay Road, Kogarah, NSW 2217
Phone Number: +61 2 9113 1111
St George Hospital offers comprehensive medical services, including emergency, surgery, and critical care.

Emergency Department at Sydney Hospital (Macquarie Street)
Address: 8 Macquarie Street, Sydney, NSW 2000
Phone Number: +61 2 9382 6111
Located in the heart of Sydney, this hospital provides emergency and urgent care services.

3. Pharmacies and Medical Assistance

Chemist Warehouse
Multiple locations throughout Sydney, including popular areas like Bondi Junction and George Street.

Opening Hours: Typically open 7 AM to 10 PM Chemist Warehouse is a well-known pharmacy chain where you can purchase over-the-counter medications, personal care products, and health supplies.

Priceline **Pharmacy**

Available across Sydney, including major shopping centers like Westfield Bondi Junction and Pitt Street Mall.

Opening Hours: Generally 8 AM to 9 PM

Another large pharmacy chain offering a range of health products, prescription refills, and health advice.

---

4. Medical Insurance and Travel Clinics

For visitors from overseas, it's highly recommended to have travel insurance that covers health-related incidents during your trip to Sydney. Additionally, if you're feeling unwell or need a check-up, you can visit a travel clinic.

Sydney **Travel** **Clinic**

Address: 37 York Street, Sydney, NSW 2000

Phone **Number**: +61 2 9223 3288

This clinic provides vaccinations, travel health advice, and medical services for international travelers.

Bupa **Medical** **Centre**

Address: 60 Margaret Street, Sydney, NSW 2000

Phone **Number**: +61 2 9211 0800

Bupa Medical Centre offers health check-ups, travel health services, and general practice care for visitors.

5. COVID-19 Related Healthcare Services

If you need a COVID-19 test or vaccination while in Sydney, there are several facilities available to assist you:

COVID-19 Testing Centers: Available at various locations around the city, many drive-thru and walk-in clinics are operational. The New South Wales (NSW) Government provides a list of locations on their official website.

Vaccination Centers: You can receive a COVID-19 vaccination at major pharmacies or designated vaccination hubs in Sydney. The NSW Health website lists vaccination locations and booking details.

---

6. Dentist and Dental Services

If you need dental care during your trip, there are many clinics throughout Sydney offering both general dentistry and emergency dental services.

Sydney CBD Dental
Address: 160 Clarence Street, Sydney, NSW 2000
Phone Number: +61 2 9262 3500
This clinic provides a range of dental services, including check-ups, fillings, and emergency treatments.

Dental on Park
Address: 46-48 Park Road, Kirribilli, NSW 2061

Phone Number: +61 2 9929 5722
Known for providing high-quality, patient-focused dental care.

---

7. Public Health Services

The **New South Wales Health Department** offers a range of public health services and information:

NSW Health Website: www.health.nsw.gov.au
The official health department website provides information on hospitals, medical services, and health alerts. You can also find guidelines on mental health, vaccination, and healthcare rights.

Conclusion

In case of any emergency or health concerns while you're in Sydney, the city has excellent healthcare facilities and services available to ensure you receive prompt and professional care. Whether you need urgent medical attention, a visit to a pharmacy, or travel health services, you'll have access to reliable healthcare providers. Always remember to have travel insurance that covers health-related incidents, and don't hesitate to reach out for help in any emergency.

10.4 Local Laws and Regulations in Sydney

When traveling to a new city, it's important to understand and respect local laws and regulations to ensure a safe and enjoyable stay. Sydney, being a major city in Australia, follows laws that are generally consistent across the country. Below are some key laws and rules to keep in mind during your visit.

1. Smoking Laws

Public Smoking: Smoking is banned in many public places, including indoor restaurants, bars, enclosed shopping malls, public transport, and within a certain distance of public entrances. Sydney also has designated smoking areas in outdoor spaces, but it is best to look out for signage indicating smoking zones.

E-Cigarettes: The use of e-cigarettes (vaping) is also regulated and subject to similar restrictions as traditional cigarettes.

2. Littering and Environmental Laws

Littering: It is illegal to litter in Sydney. Fines can be imposed if you are caught discarding rubbish on the streets or in public places. Make sure to use the bins available in public spaces.

Recycling: Sydney, like much of Australia, takes recycling seriously. You'll find separate bins for general waste and recyclables in many areas. Be sure to follow the recycling guidelines provided by the city.

3. Noise Regulations

Quiet Hours: Sydney has noise regulations to ensure that residents aren't disturbed by excessive noise, particularly during the late hours. Noise from parties, construction, or any loud activities must be kept to a minimum, especially between 10 PM and 7 AM.

4. Jaywalking and Road Rules

Pedestrian Rules: Sydney is very pedestrian-friendly, but jaywalking (crossing the road outside of designated crosswalks or against traffic lights) is illegal. Always use pedestrian crossings and wait for traffic signals to turn green.

Road Safety: If you're driving, remember that in Australia, people drive on the left side of the road. Seat belts are mandatory for all passengers, and mobile phones should not be used while driving unless you have a hands-free device.

5. Drug Laws

Illegal Drugs: The possession, use, and trafficking of illegal drugs are against the law in Sydney and the rest of Australia. The penalties for drug offenses can be severe, including fines, imprisonment, or both.

6. Wildlife and Nature Laws

Wildlife Protection: Sydney is home to many species of wildlife, and the local government enforces laws to protect animals and their habitats. Avoid feeding wildlife or disturbing protected species in national parks and coastal areas.

10.5 Currency, Tipping, and Taxes in Sydney

1. Currency

Currency Used: The official currency of Sydney and Australia is the **Australian Dollar (AUD)**. Banknotes come in denominations of $5, $10, $20, $50, and $100, while coins are available in $1, $2, 5c, 10c, 20c, and 50c.

Exchanging Currency: You can exchange foreign currency at airports, banks, or currency exchange kiosks throughout Sydney. However, be mindful that exchange rates may vary. ATMs are also widely available if you need to withdraw Australian dollars from your credit or debit card.

2. Credit Cards and Payments

Card Payments: Credit and debit cards (Visa, MasterCard, American Express) are widely accepted in Sydney, including at hotels, restaurants, shops, and taxis. Contactless payments are also common, and you can use your smartphone or card for "tap and go" payments.

Mobile Payments: Mobile payment methods such as Apple Pay, Google Pay, and Samsung Pay are accepted at many locations, so you can use your mobile phone for purchases.

3. Tipping in Sydney

Tipping Culture: While tipping is not compulsory in Sydney, it is appreciated for good service, especially in restaurants, cafes, and bars. The typical tip is around **10-15%** of the total bill.

Restaurants: In higher-end restaurants, service charges of 10-15% may be added to the bill, so be sure to check your receipt before tipping. For smaller cafes and casual dining spots, tipping is optional but still appreciated if the service was exceptional.

Taxis and Rideshare: Tipping taxi drivers or rideshare drivers is not expected, but rounding up the fare to the nearest dollar or leaving a small tip for great service is common.

4. Goods and Services Tax (GST)

GST Overview: The **Goods and Services Tax (GST)** is a 10% tax applied to most goods and services in Australia. This is included in the price of most items you buy in Sydney, so the price you see is the price you pay.

Tax Refund for Tourists: Visitors who spend over a certain amount on eligible goods in Australia can apply for a **Tax Refund Scheme (TRS)** when leaving the country. You must have receipts for the goods, and the items should be exported unused. The refund is usually processed at the airport upon departure.

5. Custom Regulations

Duty-Free Allowances: When returning to your home country, be aware of duty-free allowances. If you exceed the limit for tobacco, or other goods, you may need to pay customs duty upon arrival in your home country. Each country has different customs regulations, so it's best to check the rules before purchasing large quantities of items.

Bringing Goods into Australia: There are strict rules about bringing food, plant, and animal products into Australia to protect the country from pests and diseases. Be sure to declare any items when you pass through customs. Failure to declare restricted items can result in fines or confiscation of goods.

Conclusion

Sydney is a vibrant and welcoming city with clear laws and regulations that aim to protect residents, visitors, and the environment. By respecting the local customs, understanding currency and tipping practices, and being aware of taxes and fees, you can have a hasslefree and enjoyable visit to this exciting city. Whether you are dining out, shopping, or exploring, keeping these tips in mind will ensure a smooth and safe trip.

Printed in Dunstable, United Kingdom